Dance About Anything

Dance About Anything

Marty Sprague, MA

Helene Scheff, RDE

Susan McGreevy-Nichols

HUMAN KINETICS

Library of Congress Cataloging-in-Publication Data

Sprague, Marty, 1950-
    Dance about anything / Marty Sprague, Helene Scheff, Susan McGreevy-Nichols.
    p. cm.
    Includes bibliographical references.
    ISBN 0-7360-3000-X (soft cover)
    1. Dance--Study and teaching--Handbooks, manuals, etc. 2. Lesson planning--Handbooks,
manuals, etc. I. Scheff, Helene, 1939- II. McGreevy-Nichols, Susan, 1952- III. Title.
    GV1589.S78   2006
    792.8071--dc22

                                                            2005030225
ISBN-10: 0-7360-3000-X
ISBN-13: 978-0-7360-3000-7

Acquisitions Editor: Judy Patterson Wright, PhD; **Developmental Editor:** Amy Stahl;
Assistant Editors: Derek Campbell, Bethany J. Bentley; **Copyeditor:** Jan Feeney; **Proof-
reader:** Pam Johnson; **Permission Manager:** Dalene Reeder; **Graphic Designer:** Nancy
Rasmus; **Graphic Artist:** Angela K. Snyder; **Photo Manager:** Sarah Ritz; **Cover Designer:**
Keith Blomberg; **Photographer (interior):** Photos by Marty Sprague, except where other-
wise noted. Photos on pp. 17, 53, 68, 109, 112, and 177 by Oriana Pinheiro. Photo on
p. 141 by Lisa Scheff. **Art Manager:** Kelly Hendren; **Illustrator:** Tim Offenstein; **Printer:**
United Graphics

Printed in the United States of America

10 9 8 7 6 5 4 3 2 1

Human Kinetics
Web site: www.HumanKinetics.com

United States: Human Kinetics
P.O. Box 5076
Champaign, IL 61825-5076
800-747-4457
e-mail: humank@hkusa.com

Canada: Human Kinetics
475 Devonshire Road Unit 100
Windsor, ON N8Y 2L5
800-465-7301 (in Canada only)
e-mail: orders@hkcanada.com

Europe: Human Kinetics
107 Bradford Road
Stanningley
Leeds LS28 6AT, United Kingdom
+44 (0) 113 255 5665
e-mail: hk@hkeurope.com

Australia: Human Kinetics
57A Price Avenue
Lower Mitcham, South Australia 5062
08 8277 1555
e-mail: liaw@hkaustralia.com

New Zealand: Human Kinetics
Division of Sports Distributors NZ Ltd.
P.O. Box 300 226 Albany
North Shore City
Auckland
0064 9 448 1207
e-mail: info@humankinetics.co.nz

Contents

Part I   Inspiration   13

From Selecting Topics to Creating Short Movement Phrases

Part II   Dance Designing   45

From Solving Movement Problems to Exhibition

Preface

Dance moves! Dance is alive! You can make dance and movement a working part of anything you teach. Moving is appealing to students. Many of us doodle, swing our feet, or fidget during a lecture. Through all that moving, we are actually anchoring the learning in our brains (Hannaford, 1995). We could and should use dance as a basic way to teach and learn. Dance is a perfect tool for real-life application of educational theories. Anyone can use this book as a way to garner excitement about integrated projects with dance as a component. While the topic of this book is integrated projects, we are dance educators and are strong believers that dance should be included in all integrated teaching and learning. One of the purposes of integrated projects is to provide learning opportunities for all types of learners, and that includes the kinesthetic learner. We wrote this book to help *all* teachers, regardless of their subject areas, learn that working together as a team gets students to learn and enjoy learning. Students get to be part of the process. You can see their satisfaction as they succeed and achieve.

Dance learning is letting the body teach the brain, letting the physical inform the cognitive. In education, dance can be used in a variety of ways:

- Dance can be taught as a specific arts discipline.
- Dance can help you teach other subject areas.
- Dance can be taught through integrated projects.
- Other core subjects can be taught through dance.

In an integrated project, dance can be the major focus driving the work in all subject areas. Our integrated project of Anna and the King, shown in its entirety in chapter 13, serves as one of the examples that demonstrate how dance can drive different parts of an integrated project. Dance can also play a lesser role in an integrated project. In the Community Quilt, found in chapter 12, dance is used to introduce the idea of community. Dance is then included in the exhibition segment of the integrated project. More often, the arts are considered core subjects, and there is more focus on including arts in the classroom. Using movement and dance is also a cost-effective way of enhancing core curriculum while also deepening students' learning experiences.

We have written this book to help all teachers help their students learn in different ways. This can become a most exciting part of your educational plan. Current trends in education are requiring all teachers (physical educators, arts educators, and classroom teachers) to collaborate and integrate content from their disciplines. Many educators are at a loss about how to accomplish this. *Dance About Anything* addresses that need. The arts have always been about creating and assessing. The experts in the field of education are now turning to the arts for help in the areas of critical thinking, creative thinking, applied learning, and assessment. *Dance About Anything* will help you understand the role dance can play in integrated learning. As dance making occurs, you and your students will discover that a choreographer creates moving images for the audience that express an idea, concept, emotion, or story line.

We have had extensive experience in making dances and creating and implementing integrated projects in the public school setting. The school in which we taught was famous for semester-long integrated projects. In addition to drawing an audience of 3,500, these projects involved at least 400 student performers. Often, 8 to 10 faculty members from a variety of subject areas facilitated and taught. With the help of this book, you can learn how to make this happen in your setting as well. Integrated projects don't have to last a whole semester. You can start small and expand the projects as you gain confidence and a following in your school. We have also made presentations on the topic of integrated projects at many local and national workshops and conferences. We have heard reports from conference and workshop participants (teachers of grades K to 12) that they went home, tried the projects, and modified them with great success.

We have developed a progression of movement activities, from dance designing activities through integrated project plans. This progression increases in complexity from the moment of initial inspiration through the exhibition of the integrated project. In this book, inspiration is considered a single idea that develops and becomes a simple movement phrase. The outlined progression gives you, your colleagues, and your students confidence and experience in using dance in the classroom. Dance designing, the second phase, includes the development, revision, and performance of a dance. When complete, integration takes you from an initial idea through the design, revision, implementation, and exhibition of an integrated project. The bound-in CD-ROM has many worksheets, handouts, and blank activity forms. You can use these documents as they are or tailor them to your and your students' needs. This is all about student learning and how we, as educators, can enhance and facilitate the learning process at any level.

Integrating means to bring together or incorporate parts into a whole. In integrated projects, various subject areas are brought together and the learning is approached as a whole. For example, a study can be made of the community in which the school is located. Social studies, geography, visual arts, music, folk art, English language arts, economics, teamwork, home and consumer science, and of course dance are part of the whole integrated project. The student learning is not segmented by subject areas; rather, it flows freely from subject area to subject area as the work requires. To complete the project work and products, students combine skills and concepts from all subject areas.

From this book, you will learn how dance fits into integrated projects in different ways. It is interesting to note that dance occurs at very different times in these integrated projects. Sometimes the major dance product is created at the end of the integrated project, as you will see in the Community Quilt integrated project. In the Anna and the King integrated project, the dance designing occurs immediately after researching and identifying important aspects of the topic, and it drives all the work in other subject areas.

Integrated dance projects can be created to meet standards, cover curricular content, connect subject areas, and meet student needs. In *Building More Dances* (McGreevy-Nichols, Scheff, & Sprague, 2001) we discussed how to align your curriculum with standards. Use this alignment strategy, but before beginning your integrated project, you need to check with your school district regarding which local, district, state, and national standards are being used.

Using dance in the classroom is fun. You and your colleagues have a new way to look at your areas of expertise and a new way to approach teaching and learning. The staleness, repetition, and general malaise of teaching the same content the same way all the time goes out the window and you are refreshed. Even better, students stay engaged with the learning process, and the students can move about to show what they have learned. No longer are they bound to their desks, reiterating what they have learned only by writing. The parents and your other colleagues have proof, in viewing the exhibition and seeing the work in the portfolios, that the children have gained knowledge, can apply it, and can demonstrate their capabilities. Everyone has a good time, much learning takes place, and the results are usually terrific!

How to Use This Book and CD-ROM

You can use *Dance About Anything* in a variety of ways. You can take different paths to achieve the goal of an integrated project. You can add your creativity and that of your students to the mix to make this truly *your* work. This book follows the creative progression of an integrated project from inspiration to dance design to exhibition of the completed project. Through the use of this book and all the ancillary information on the CD-ROM, you will have a firm grasp on working with integrated projects and making them work for you and your students.

The chapters in parts I and II describe the choreographic process specifically for the creation of a dance, including inspiration and dance designing activities. You will need this information to impart knowledge to your students so that they, too, can be part of the dance-making process. Part III uses the creative process for the creation and implementation of an integrated project plan. Here again, teaching and learning are student centered; you, being the team leader, keep the project up and running. Part IV provides you with three complete integrated project plans to use with your students. How closely you follow the plans or how much you change them is totally up to you and the working team you gather.

Introduction to Integrated Projects

We start our book with an introduction section that gives a solid foundation on which the rest of the book is based. This introduction gives support for the fact that good thinking is fundamental to all learning. In a basic thinking process, there are seven stages—or, as we call them, tasks—that should be used. In other words, "the process is the process." We give you a comparison of the cognitive processes and relate them to one another so that you and your students can begin to understand the thinking process in order to create something new. For instance, if the topic is the growth cycle of plants, the concept task in the creative process is to show the seed growing and unfurling into a plant. The scientific process would ask the question "What is needed in order for a seed to grow?" The problem-solving process would ask the question "How can we grow the healthiest plant possible?" The writing process could identify the topic as the growth cycle and how it relates to the writer's own development. Additionally in the introduction, we introduce you to the creative process, which we cross-reference to the choreographic process. You also will discover that integrating the arts into the classroom has a positive effect on learning and is supported by educational theory. Finally, no dance education book would be complete without ways to assess outcomes, so we give you a plan for assessment as well. Reading and digesting this chapter will prepare you for the fun work that starts with chapter 1.

Establishing the Tasks of the Choreographic Process

The first three parts of this book introduce, or reintroduce, you to the seven tasks of the creative process. Part I, Inspiration: From Selecting Topics to Creating Short Movement Phrases (chapters 1 to 3), introduces you to the beginnings of the creative process and explains how you can develop movement phrases from almost any beginning inspiration. A general topic of flight is used as an example to illustrate how to initiate the first three tasks of the creative process (including the concept task, investigation task, and exploration task) in three different grade levels: K to 4, 5 to 8, and 9 to 12. (These appear as sidebars in the text or tables at the end of each chapter in part I. You can use these examples of flight as is or you can use them as a reference while you create your own inspiration activities using the templates on the CD-ROM.) No one knows better than you the capabilities of your students. You can use these defined grade levels, or you can adjust the sample inspiration activities to the needs of you and your students. You are given some suggestions of topics for generating movement phrases. These suggestions take the form of Inspiration Activity

Cards in chapter 3. These cards can be used as a game in which a clue is given on one side of the card. Students can pick a card, or you can hand them a card. When the card is flipped over, they will find written instructions to follow.

Part II, Dance Designing: From Solving Movement Problems to Exhibition (chapters 4 to 6), takes you through the remaining tasks of the creative process, including the selection task, development task, refinement task, and exhibition task. In part II, you will also be introduced to Dance Designing Activity Cards, which take the students through the critical-thinking and movement processes of designing a dance. Again, the topic of flight is used as an example in sidebars for all three grade levels. The dance designing activities state what student work is expected. Instructions explain how the work can be accomplished, and dance designing suggestions are listed. Students are referred to handouts that can aid them. Your students can look at these cards as a puzzle that needs to be solved. Again, you are bringing the students into the equation.

Part III, Integrated Projects: From Thematic Planning to Exhibition (chapters 7 to 10), gives guidance for and instruction about developing and implementing integrated projects. We further define an integrated project in chapter 7 and describe how to create such a project of your own with the use of a blank template and referral to the sample integrated projects on flight for all grade levels.

The information and time line in chapter 8 comprise the practical aspects of implementing integrated projects. You will learn how to move the project forward by taking the single inspiration through the creation of a dance and on to the exhibition of an integrated project. This chapter also discusses practical concerns about the *who* (building your team), the *what* (division of responsibilities), the *how* (some practical hints), the *when* (timing of the project work), and the *where* (information about possible venues). We provide a step-by-step guide for project completion, including a flexible time line and suggestions on how to make helpful connections within your school and community.

From chapter 9 you will learn about the strategies of teaching, coaching, and facilitating and how to know which strategy to use in engaging and maintaining student interest. Chapter 10 takes you through the process of developing the performances and exhibitions and evaluating the big picture of integrated projects.

Sample Integrated Projects

Part IV, Three Complete Themes and Integrated Projects (chapters 11 to 13), details three complete integrated projects, one for each grade level. Chapter 11, Cosmic Influences: Weather You Like It or Not, outlines a project for grades K to 4. Chapter 12, Community: Community Quilt, is appropriate for grades 5 to 8. Chapter 13, Prejudice and Human Rights: Anna and the King, is appropriate for grades 9 to 12. In most situations, you can elect to use any of the projects for any of the grade levels by adapting them to your own situations.

Student Worksheets and Handouts

In the bound-in CD-ROM you will find documents to use with your students, including Inspiration Activity Cards, Dance Designing Activity Cards, templates for Inspiration Activity Cards and Dance Designing Activity Cards, student worksheets and handouts, and assessment forms. Thumbnail figures of this material are imbedded in appropriate places in the text so that you can see where and how each piece works. You will also find a CD-ROM icon in the text each time a form that appears on the bound-in CD-ROM is first mentioned in a chapter or in one of the student work tasks in part IV. For each of the tasks described in chapters 1 through 6, there are sample worksheets that you can use with your students as you facilitate these tasks. Again, these worksheets are pictured in the text where they are first described and are found in full-size reproducible form on the CD-ROM. These worksheets will give your students plenty of opportunity to enhance their portfolios.

With this information you and your students can take an idea or inspiration, design and build dances, and make them part of integrated projects. You *can* dance about anything—from start to finish!

Acknowledgments

We wish to offer thanks to so many people who were part of our integrated projects over the years. Most of these teachers and artists were from Roger Williams Middle School in Providence, Rhode Island, and from the community at large.

Many people were involved with the projects in this book as well as others that we did over the years. They are Gerri Lallo, Linda Gilo (dance teachers); Lynn Baldwin, Patricia Huntington (art teachers); Annette Pesatauro (ELA teacher); our special team of sixth-grade teachers; and all the amazing teachers and students at Roger Williams Middle School. All of these patient and wonderful people contributed time, expertise, and energy to each of the projects. We are grateful!

We are also appreciative of the support of Ed Scheff and John Sprague and indebted to the fine people at Human Kinetics who have helped us follow our path in making dance education available to all children and their teachers. We wish to acknowledge everyone at Human Kinetics for their guidance and support, especially Judy Wright and Amy Stahl.

The Role of Dance in Integrated Projects

Throughout the years, we have observed students engaged in the choreographic process. We have watched their development as creative and critical thinkers. This growth was evident not only in dance but in other subject areas as well. Their experiences with the choreographic process allowed them to grow in other thinking processes (cognitive processes) as well. For example, we have witnessed students take the progression of tasks in the choreographic process and transfer them to the problem-solving and writing processes. Literacy-phobic students have more willingness to engage in the writing process after they have created a dance. That is because through dance they learn that the process is the process and that good thinking is fundamental to all learning.

In this introduction, we compare four **cognitive processes.** The creative process is the way you think when making something new or creating an artistic work. The scientific process is the way you think when conducting a scientific inquiry. The problem-solving process is the way you think when confronted with a dilemma or problem to be solved. The writing process is the way you think when creating a written work. There is a similar and logical progression in all four cognitive (thinking) processes. In this book, the progression takes the form of a series of seven steps, or tasks. Table I.1 aligns the tasks, making it easier to compare the cognitive processes.

Table I.1 Comparison of Cognitive Processes

Task	Creative and artistic	Scientific	Problem solving	Writing
1. Concept	Choose topic	Ask question and define problem	Define problem as a question	Identify topic
2. Investigation	Research topic	Research and collect data	Research and investigate	Do general research
3. Exploration	Identify important aspects of topic	Revelation, see a method, generalize	Get many solutions	Collect ideas, expand research
4. Selection	Devise problems to be solved, ask questions	Develop hypothesis	Choose best solution	Limit subjects
5. Development	Solve problems and produce material	Experiment or test, verify or prove false	Check validity of solution	Write first draft, self-evaluate, rewrite
6. Refinement	Design artwork, self-evaluate, revise	Write final peer evaluation	Try out solution	Do first review of final draft
7. Exhibition	Get and use feedback from performance or show	Publish response to feedback: acceptance or criticism	Get feedback and do final evaluation of solution	Publish and receive public response

Reprinted, by permission, from H. Scheff, M. Sprague, and S. McGreevy-Nichols, 2005, *Experiencing dance: From student to dance artist* (Champaign, IL: Human Kinetics), 46.

All these processes are involved in learning or making something new. Often, as teachers, we have an idea or an inspiration that we would like to make into an integrated project. By using the cognitive processes, you can build a complete integrated project. The development of the project needs to follow a logical progression to ensure good end results. The creative process can be used in creating visual art, theater, music, and dance activities. The scientific process can be used in establishing a focusing question for the integrated project and in planning activities that address the particular focusing question. The problem-solving process can help you think through any situation faced or question posed while creating or implementing the integrated project. The writing process helps you plan student assignments for the written work appropriate to the integrated project.

Using the Creative Process to Make Dances

Choreography is the art of making dances, and hence is a creative process. To the casual observer or the appreciative audience, the choreographic process seems like magic. Often it seems that the dance forms itself. As stated in the preface, the choreographer creates moving images for the audience that express an idea, topic, concept, emotion, or story line. Everyone can learn a sequence of tasks that will develop artwork. In *Building Dances* (McGreevy-Nichols, Scheff, & Sprague, 2005) and *Building More Dances* (McGreevy-Nichols, et al., 2001) we discussed seven steps to building dances—a choreographic process. These seven steps helped people to create a product—a dance.

Following is an explanation of the choreographic process as it relates to the sequence of seven tasks.

1. Concept task: A dance has to be about something. This something, or topic, could be an idea, an emotion, or even a style of expression (as in traditional dance forms).

2. Investigation task: To communicate the concept of a dance, the choreographer has to gather information or knowledge about this concept. This research could take the form of notes from typical resources (books and Internet), journals, personal observations, collection of traditional steps, or even just conversations with other people.

3. Exploration task: There has to be some sorting process, because there is usually more available information than can be used in one dance. The choreographer must decide how to make the concept of the dance pure, strong, and clear for the audience. This sorting process could even take the form of playing around with movement (improvisation) to discover which aspect of the concept produces the richest, most interesting movement.

4. Selection task: Once the best choices of aspects of the topic have been chosen, the choreographer must lay out a plan of attack, which could be set up as a movement problem. Simply stated, how can the aspect most effectively be communicated through movement? For example, if the aspect is diversity, then the choreographer could set up a section of the dance as a theme and variation. The choreographic form of theme and variation is a movement phrase or section of a dance with subsequent movement phrases or sections created as variations of the original.

5. Development task: By actually solving the movement problem or making movement that fulfills the plan for the sections, the choreographer will have generated movement phrases that act as the raw material from which the dance is to be made.

6. Refinement task: Once there is movement particularly relevant to the original concept, then the choreographer can design the dance by manipulating the movement into an arrangement or structure. Often choreographers share their new work with trusted colleagues or a small test audience before unveiling the dance to a larger audience. Based on the feedback the choreographer gets, he or she simultaneously evaluates and revises the dance. The dance is then ready to be presented to the world.

7. Exhibition task: A dance cannot exist in a vacuum. It should be presented to an audience. The audience gives feedback on the dance, either accepting it or rejecting it. If the dance is to be seen again, the choreographer will then make any needed revisions in the dance. The feedback can also be applied to the choreographer's next dance project.

The choreographic process described in this book has been developed to align with the other cognitive processes. Table I.2 shows this alignment of the sequence of tasks for the choreographic process with the creative process.

Advocacy: Supporting Educational Theory

Integrated projects that include hands-on activities appeal to people with various learning styles. In integrated projects, new

Table I.2 Artistic Choreographic Process

Task	Artistic	Choreography
1. Concept	Choose a topic.	Choose a topic.
2. Investigation	Research the topic.	Research the topic.
3. Exploration	Identify important aspects of the topic.	Identify important aspects of the topic.
4. Selection	Devise problems to be solved, ask questions.	Devise movement problems.
5. Development	Solve problems, produce material.	Solve movement problems and make movement phrases.
6. Refinement	Design artwork, self-evaluate, revise.	Design dance manipulating movement phrases. Get feedback and revise as needed.
7. Exhibition	Get and use feedback from performance	Exhibit completed dance. Accept final critique to apply to next work or to make changes for next performance of this work.

learning is placed in relevant context. Student-generated work, assessments, and even dance phrases ensure student interest and ownership. An exhibition or a performance brings this information to life, and all types of learners are given the opportunity to shine at some point during the project. Following are some educational theories that can be used for advocacy.

Multiple Intelligences

Howard Gardner has put forward his theory of multiple intelligences, which states that people have conscious and unconscious preferences in their learning styles. These multiple intelligences are verbal-linguistic, musical, logical-mathematical, visual-spatial, bodily-kinesthetic, intrapersonal, and interpersonal. Dr. Gardner developed other ways of thinking, or possible intelligences, that include observing and classifying (naturalist intelligence) and thinking spiritually or philosophically (existentialist thinking) (Gardner 1999).

Dance appeals to all of these intelligences. Following are explanations that connect dance to these different classifications of intelligences:

1. Verbal-linguistic intelligence is used during the research and assessment phases of the dance-making process. Communication during teamwork calls for clear and precise linguistic skills.

2. Musical intelligence is engaged in dance learning through the timing and rhythmic aspects inherent in dance and movement.

3. Logical-mathematical intelligence is put to use during the ordering and reordering of movement phrases and dancers, counting out of musical beats, and determining the number of movement solutions possible in a given problem.

4. Visual-spatial intelligence is used when controlling one's body in crowds while moving in a variety of situations. Manipulating other dancers when choreographing requires the use of spatial design. In dance it matters where you are at any given time because there are immediate safety and artistic consequences.

5. Bodily-kinesthetic intelligence, of course, includes dance. The use of the body as a medium for knowledge, communication, and expression allows for the use of a symbol system that is entirely different from the linguistic (word) system. Dance can express the essence of an idea without thinking in words.

6. Intrapersonal intelligence, the knowledge of ourselves, is absolutely involved in dance learning. With each new experience in dance and movement, students become more aware, more skilled, and better able to direct their own learning. They know their capabilities and their weak areas. Because dance is movement, new knowledge is immediately and holistically connected to past learning. (For more information, see the section on brain research later in this introduction.)

7. Interpersonal intelligence is used in making dances and performing by relying on teamwork and an understanding of other people.

8. Naturalist intelligence is useful in finding inspirations (making observations in the natural world) and sorting out options (categorization).

9. Existentialist intelligence is used when the students, as they are being creative, are aware of being connected to something larger than themselves.

Forms of Representation

Elliot Eisner (1982) supports the use of interdisciplinary and integrated instruction through his theory and research on forms of representation. Forms of representation can be words, pictures, music, mathematics, or dance that are used as communication devices. Eisner thinks that some concepts are better expressed through one form of representation than another. Dance and movement can actually show the dynamics of the action and changes in speed and velocity of a tornado better than words or pictures can. However, a garden of colorful flowers is better represented by a painting than by a dance. If this is true, then both movement and visual art must be available to students for the understanding and expression of certain concepts. Eisner is in agreement with Howard Gardner in what should be educationally available to children as they develop. Each type of learner should be supported and valued. Integrated projects, especially those that include the arts, provide more and varied learning opportunities than single-subject projects or activities.

Perceiving, Thinking, and Forming

Rudolf Arnheim (1983) states that the three fundamentals that education and the productive mind have in common are perceiving (understanding relationships between things), thinking, and forming. Perceiving, thinking, and forming are also basic to the choreographic (dance-making) process, wherein the dance maker perceives or is inspired by an idea, thinks through the directing of the movement and dancers, and forms or creates a dance. Similarly, integrated projects call for students to perceive the main ideas or concepts of the project, think through plans for the learning product, and form this learning product. The creation of a new product by using thinking processes that span all subject areas and using skills and concepts from many different subject areas help students to make connections across the curricula and to their own lives.

Brain Research

In the past few years, there has been much exciting research in brain functioning and structure. New understanding of how the brain perceives, sorts, stores, and retrieves information has reformed teaching and learning strategies. Following is some supporting information on brain research and its implications for education. This information is helpful in holding students' attention during the learning process.

In order for something to be meaningful, at least one of the following must be present: relevance, emotion, or context. According to Jensen (1998), relevance occurs within the brain when the brain is able to make a connection to existing neural networks (prior knowledge). Emotions are then triggered by the chemicals that are released when these preexisting neural networks are activated. Long-term memory is more easily attained when emotions are attached to the memory. Putting information in a context allows for pattern making that may cause the formation or activation of larger neural fields. The teacher's job is designing complex student work that requires the brain to pull into action enough neural networks to create meaning, learning, and long-term memory: the goal of education. Students will then have a chance to increase their knowledge and produce better work.

Cooperative teamwork and the teacher's facilitation of an emotionally safe work environment can support learning. Cooperative group work can also provide emotional and contextual memory prompts that may make the learned content easier to retrieve.

One helpful finding from brain research is that certain positive experiences can change body chemistry and aid in the learning and problem-solving process.

> Exercise and positive social contacts, such as hugging, music, and the supportive comments of friends, can elevate endorphin levels and thus make us feel good about ourselves and our social environment (Levinthal, 1988). Joyful classroom environments that encourage such behaviors create an internal chemical response that can increase the possibility that students will learn how to solve problems successfully in potentially stressful situations. (Sylwester, 2000, p. 38)

With the support of this quotation, it is easy to see how dance, which engages the cognitive, emotional, and physical aspects of a person, can help students better use their minds in stressful situations. This is another goal of education.

As previously stated, emotion ensures that humans remember information and may also ensure that humans remember that information with more vividness. Indeed, many of our students have returned years later with memories of their integrated projects and performances. The concepts that they portrayed physically and emotionally in their performances seem to have been deeply ingrained in their memories. These same former students say that the thinking skills that they learned to use in these projects have proved useful in their lives after the middle school years.

In support of these rather anecdotal findings, Joseph Ledoux (1996, p. 206) states the following:

> This [type of research] suggests that if adrenaline [epinephrine] is released naturally (from the adrenal gland) in some situation, that experience will be remembered especially well. Since emotional arousal usually results in the release of adrenaline, it might be expected that explicit conscious memory of emotional situations would be stronger than the explicit memory of non-emotional situations.

As stated by Patricia Wolfe (2001, p. 134), "Simulations that take advantage of the mind-body connection are powerful tools for retention and understanding." Integrated projects that incorporate dance and the creative process involve much more than simple role-playing activities. Since the connection between mind and body is inherent in dance, as noted in the earlier section on multiple intelligences, the learning has to be deeper and more meaningful for students.

According to Wolfe (2001, p. 107), "Solving real-life problems is another way to raise the emotional and motivational stakes." John Dewey (1934) put forth that education should be more experiential and about real life. To ensure student engagement, integrated projects should address real-life issues that are relevant to the students and to the community.

If "learning is a process of building neural networks" (Wolfe, 2001, p. 135), then it is ideal to engage as many senses as we can in the learning process. Dance engages all the senses. When students dance about something, learning is not passive. Dance moves and has an emotional content involving so many more neural pathways than rote learning involves. When certain skills and concepts seem to be difficult for students, brain research shows that as the amount of sensory input in the experience increases, "the more intricate will be the patterns for learning, thought, and creativity" (Hannaford, 1995, p. 30). For example, the sense of touch can be employed to help students understand the qualities of movement (e.g., a feather or cotton balls represent lightness and the rope used in a tug-of-war represents strength).

How deep is dance learning and how long does it last? The following is a true story. A 28-year-old man, then serving in the air force in the military police, visits his old middle school. While talking to the dance teacher, he is asked, "What do you remember?" He begins to list names of dances and special groups of dancers with whom he performed. After being shown four beats of movement from a dance he had learned 17 years earlier, he physically tenses and tears come to his eyes. He repeats over and over, "I remember! I remember! I can't believe I remember!"

Assessment

Assessing integrated projects is not unlike assessing any other student work. The major difference is that instead of one piece of work, an integrated project is composed of many pieces of work that are linked by a common theme and that hinge on one another. Student work in the project ranges from the simple, such as a list of research sources, to the more complex, such as a lecture/demonstration. A student's work needs to be acknowledged in some way. Work that is valued by the teacher is in turn valued by the student. Acknowledgment of student work can be as simple as a check-off indicating that a student has completed the assignment, or it can be as complex as a precise score that was calculated with the use of a detailed rubric. Your choice on how to score the piece is determined by the importance and complexity of the work. A good rule to follow is that if the piece of work meets multiple standards, then create a rubric for it. If the work is part of the process for a larger piece of work, then a rubric is not necessary and a check-off is all that is needed.

Assessments of the more complex pieces of work start with clear criteria. Criteria define the piece of work and come from the following sources:

- Standards and specific benchmarks (this is nonnegotiable)
- Specific curricular content
- Student input
- Class protocol
- Exemplars

After identifying the criteria, create a rubric. A rubric takes the criteria and assigns a value to it. Rubrics should always have a value assigned for having satisfactorily completed all criteria (at standard) and a value for completing aspects above and beyond the criteria (above standard). This value is the grade or score to be given to the work. Sample values for student work include the following scales:

- 5 to 1 (5 being the highest score possible and 1 being the lowest possible)
- +, ✓, −
- A, B, C, D, F (not recommended for standards-based grading)

A tool that can be used to guide the student through the assessment process is a student work form. The student work form lists the standards, describes the student work, provides instructions for completing the work, and includes a rubric. This form serves two purposes. First, it tells the students what is expected from them (this document is written to the student). Second, it can serve as a cover sheet that states the grade and completes the documentation of the work. Form I.1, Student Work Form, on the CD-ROM contains a template.

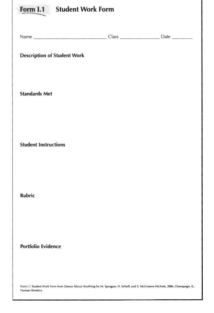

Form I.1 Student Work Form

Name _____ Class _____ Date _____

Description of Student Work

Standards Met

Student Instructions

Rubric

Portfolio Evidence

Form I.1 Student Work Form from *Dance About Anything* by M. Sprague, H. Scheff, and S. McGreevy-Nichols, 2006, Champaign, IL: Human Kinetics.

Assessment is not limited to the completed piece of work. A great amount of student learning occurs during the process of carrying out a piece of rigorous student work. The process produces important evidence that students have met standards, and this process should be documented. This documentation can be accomplished through a process portfolio, which provides a powerful summary of student learning. Student thinking, as well as the "baby steps" taken, can be carefully documented within the process portfolio through the use of videotaped exercises and activities, journals, draft documents, and worksheets. Note that when using video, you may need to have a video and photography release form signed by students' parents or guardians. Check with your principal for your school's rule on this matter.

Summary

In this introduction we discuss the cognitive processes—creative, problem-solving, writing, and scientific—and how they can be compared to one another. The tables also help you to see those comparisons. We give you an overview of educational theory and how dance is a perfect vehicle for learning. There is a section on how to assess large and small pieces of student work. With this overview, you can begin the process of creating an integrated project.

Part I

Inspiration
From Selecting Topics to Creating Short Movement Phrases

In part I we introduce you to the first three tasks of the choreographic process: choosing a topic (Concept Task, chapter 1), researching the topic (Investigation Task, chapter 2), and identifying important aspects of the topic (Exploration Task, chapter 3). These tasks are the basis for creating the movement phrases, which are the products of our inspiration activities.

Also in part I you will find a description of how to begin the creative and choreographic processes. You will learn how to take your students on the journey of learning through movement. The students might contribute their own inspirations as the seed for the concept or topic, or you might discover your own inspirations for movement activities. In either case, you will find that the creation of a movement phrase can lead to enthusiasm for making dances and for learning new things.

At the end of part (pp. 42-44) I you will find copies of the Flight Inspiration Activities. They appear as tables (tables 3.2, 3.3, and 3.4) highlighting the first three tasks of the cognitive processes.

Chapter 1

Concept Task: Choosing a Topic

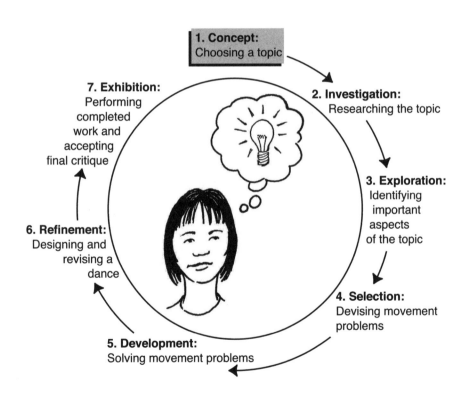

1. **Concept:** Choosing a topic

2. **Investigation:** Researching the topic

3. **Exploration:** Identifying important aspects of the topic

4. **Selection:** Devising movement problems

5. **Development:** Solving movement problems

6. **Refinement:** Designing and revising a dance

7. **Exhibition:** Performing completed work and accepting final critique

Questions that are consistently asked of us at workshops are "Where do you get your ideas for your dances and integrated projects?" and "Where does your inspiration come from?" The answers are "Anywhere, everywhere, and all around us!" Inspirations can originate from anything. Think about common items that you may use every day, such as a broom or a chair. Look out the window and perhaps you will see a bird or an airplane, which could bring to mind the concept of flight. A colleague is teaching immigration in his social studies class, and this could remind you of your grandmother, who told you stories of your ancestors. Water dripping from the faucet could inspire you to represent H_2O for a science activity by linking up one movement (done twice) with a different movement.

Everyday Inspirations

At one time we were conducting many off-site workshops and we needed to come up with a surefire way of engaging our substitute teachers, who had little or no knowledge of dance. We knew they

You can truly dance about anything, anywhere.

needed to feel comfortable with what we were asking them to do. We started by looking around our office. We gathered books and magazines on a variety of subjects, puppets, objects with which you can make sounds, music, fabrics, furniture, picture postcards, cafeteria trays, masks, calendars, videos, games, and costume pieces. We left simple instructions with our collection of items. The students, in small teams, were to choose an item from our collection and create movement inspired by the chosen item. All that the substitute teacher had to do was to deliver the instructions and facilitate the students' work. These movement activities were a success. The substitute teachers felt in control while teaching an unfamiliar discipline, and the students created wonderful movement phrases.

Soon, no matter where we were, we found ourselves writing our inspirations on restaurant napkins and scraps of paper; finally we started to write these inspirations in a journal, which we carried with us at all times. Inspirations occurred to us at unexpected times: during conversations with students and colleagues and while walking in malls, riding in cars, flying in airplanes, and even sitting in meetings. We recorded these inspirations on individual

Inspiration can come from anything lying around, even big circles.

cards so that we could easily hand them out to students. The phrase "make a card" became part of our daily conversations.

After your next meeting, check the doodles on your notepad to see which ones would make good inspirations (see figure 1.1). As an example of this "anytime or anything" aspect of inspiration, while on a plane traveling to a conference, we thought that the description of safety procedures and the emergency exit procedure card would be a great inspiration for dance movement. Next time you fly in a plane, take the time to read the emergency exit procedure card. Pull out the verbs and envision using the movements as dance movement. Observe the flight attendants as they demonstrate the emergency procedures. The gestures for locating the exits and using the oxygen masks are certainly inspirations for movement explorations.

You can take inspirations from any of the following:

- Pictures. A work of art by Norman Rockwell, with the family as the center, could be the inspiration for the topic of families and their relationships.

- Everyday objects, such as brooms, chairs, and cafeteria trays. These three items can inspire a discussion of the use of everyday objects for unconventional purposes, as in the 1960s art scene or in abstract art. An example is Andy Warhol's use of the tomato soup can as an inspiration for his painting.

- Current, historical, and social events. These events could inspire marches and gatherings for awareness of community or historical causes.

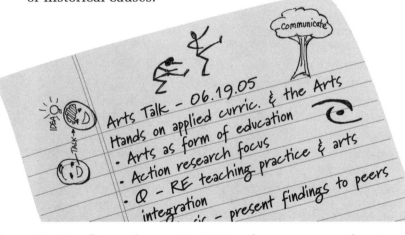

Figure 1.1 Doodles can become inspirations for movement exploration.

- Sight, sound, touch, smell, and taste. A bag full of soft items such as feathers, cotton balls, or fake fur could inspire young children to explore moving softly and lightly.
- Emotions and feelings. Choosing emotions such as happiness and joy could lead to the topic of important events during a person's life cycle.
- Printed materials. Articles or books on discrimination could suggest a study on diversity.

As for creating your own ideas, the sky is the limit. Get a cardboard box. As you see and find objects, magazine articles, stories, pictures, and any ideas or things that catch your attention, throw them into the "inspiration box" or make a card. These inspirations can be used as concepts or topics from which students generate movement. Often we would show an item to the class and ask them to tell us what and how that item inspired the students. They even formed working groups by self-dividing according to similar inspirations. Students can create their own list of inspirations by using form 1.1, Inspiration From Words and Icons. An explanation of how to use the concept task worksheets appears at the end of this chapter.

Inspirations From Classroom Content

Another inspiration for concepts or topics can be classroom content or curricular themes. Many schools require that certain topics be covered in certain grades. Some examples are the family in kindergarten, weather in the third grade, the rain forest in the fourth grade, world cultures in the sixth grade, and conflict and resolution in the eighth grade. When the family is used as a topic, some of the subtopics can include celebrating holidays, taking a trip, and greeting and including new family members. Subtopics of weather could be the weather patterns in your geographic area, how the weather patterns affect what students do and how they feel, and each student's favorite season. At the high school level, themes such as power and corruption can cross the boundaries of subject areas. An example of this theme would be World War II, Nazis, and the Holocaust, which can combine literature and history.

When working on an integrated project with a team of sixth-grade teachers, we used a systematic approach. Looking at a period of time during the school year, we shared what the students should be studying in each of the subject areas. As a group, we then came up with an overarching theme. Three examples of these themes were the mystery of the missing tectonic plate, a trip through the solar system, and fractured folk tales. All dances and other pieces of student work were derived from these inspirations.

Themes can often emerge from simple inspirations, such as observing birds flying (see table 1.1). This simple inspiration leads to the overarching theme of flight. The larger theme is worthy of a complete integrated project (see table 7.1 on page 97).

Activities for Inspiration

You can use the eight Inspiration Activity Cards (forms 3.8 to 3.15) on the CD-ROM that are a basis for short movement explorations,

Table 1.1   Flight Inspiration Activity As It Relates to Tasks of Choreographic Process (Grades K to 4)

Task	Inspiration activity
Concept task	Inspiration activity: Flight (grades K to 4) Clue: Come fly with me! **Topic or source of inspiration: Observing birds flying**
Investigation task (observe, come up with ideas)	Instructions: 1. Look at photos or video clips of birds flying. 2. Come up with a list of words describing the various aspects of flight.
Exploration task (categories)	3. Sort words that are similar in meaning into categories. (An example of a category for the inspiration of a track meet might be types of races; another might be events in which you throw something.) 4. Choose 4 or 5 words from your favorite category. 5. Create a movement signature (an identifying movement or short series of movements) for each of the words. 6. Combine all your movement signatures into one movement phrase. Your movement will look like a bird in flight.
	You are creating a simple movement phrase. A movement phrase is a dance sentence.

as explained in the section titled Using the Inspiration Activity Cards on page 40 in chapter 3. Each inspiration activity on the enclosed CD-ROM can produce a collection of original movements and movement phrases by following the first three steps in the process for creating an integrated project. In a class of 26 students, you could find 26 different movement phrases from one inspiration. Remember that the topic is the *what* that you are trying to explore or communicate. Whether it is a single word or a complex theme, the topic is your inspiration for creating. There is no right or wrong conclusion when you're following an inspiration, and this process could even let you move outward to a new topic.

Using the Concept Task Worksheets

The purpose of the worksheets for the concept task is to help you find topics and concepts for inspiration. There is a worksheet that you can adapt for each of the grade levels according to the needs of your students.

- Form 1.1, Inspiration From Words and Icons, includes icons that illustrate the printed word.

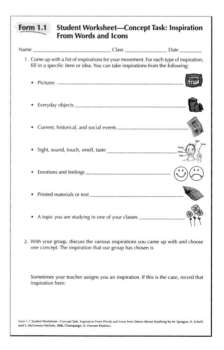

- Form 1.2, Inspiration From Words, uses the same form without the icons.

Form 1.2 Student Worksheet—Concept Task: Inspiration From Words

Name _____ Class _____ Date _____

1. Come up with a list of inspirations for your movement. For each type of inspiration, fill in a specific item or idea. You can take inspirations from the following:

- Pictures _____

- Everyday objects _____

- Current, historical, and social events _____

- Sight, sound, touch, smell, taste _____

- Emotions and feelings _____

- Printed materials or text _____

- A topic you are studying in one of your classes _____

2. With your group, discuss the various inspirations you came up with and choose one concept. The inspiration that our group has chosen is

Sometimes your teacher assigns you an inspiration. If this is the case, record that inspiration here:

Form 1.2 Student Worksheet—Concept Task: Inspiration From Words from *Dance About Anything* by M. Sprague, H. Scheff, and S. McGreevy-Nichols, 2006, Champaign, IL: Human Kinetics.

- Form 1.3, Inspiration Journal, uses the Inspiration Journal taken from lesson 9.1 in our student textbook *Experiencing Dance* (2005). A rubric is included with this form.

Form 1.3 Student Worksheet—Concept Task: Inspiration Journal

Name _____ Class _____ Date _____

Instructions: As you see, feel, hear, experience, and think of ideas or inspirations for dances, write them in the spaces provided. Be sure to explain why this inspiration or idea might make a good dance. (If you are creating a dance with a small group, share these brainstorm ideas with your choreography project team members.)

Rubric and Grading:

(+) = More than 12 inspirations or ideas are written. All inspirations or ideas are backed up by at least one supporting reason.

(√) = At least 10 inspirations or ideas are written. All inspirations or ideas are backed up by at least one supporting reason.

(-) = Fewer than 10 inspirations or ideas are written and/or inspirations or ideas are missing supporting reasons.

1. Inspiration:

   Reasons this might make a good dance:

2. Inspiration:

   Reasons this might make a good dance:

3. Inspiration:

   Reasons this might make a good dance:

4. Inspiration:

   Reasons this might make a good dance:

(continued)

Form 1.3 Student Worksheet—Concept Task: Inspiration Journal from *Dance About Anything* by M. Sprague, H. Scheff, and S. McGreevy-Nichols, 2006, Champaign, IL: Human Kinetics. Reprinted, by permission, from H. Scheff, M. Sprague, and S. McGreevy-Nichols, 2005, *Experiencing Dance: From Student to Dance Artist Instructor Guide* (Champaign, IL: Human Kinetics).

Reprinted, by permission, from H. Scheff, M. Sprague, and S. McGreevy-Nichols, 2005, *Experiencing dance: From student to dance artist instructor guide* (Champaign, IL: Human Kinetics).

Chapter 2

Investigation Task: Researching the Topic

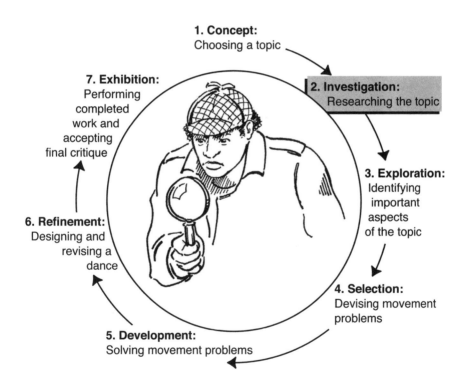

1. **Concept:** Choosing a topic

2. **Investigation:** Researching the topic

3. **Exploration:** Identifying important aspects of the topic

4. **Selection:** Devising movement problems

5. **Development:** Solving movement problems

6. **Refinement:** Designing and revising a dance

7. **Exhibition:** Performing completed work and accepting final critique

This chapter provides basic information about the investigation task, specifically about what constitutes research, and, with the help of the worksheets provided, how you facilitate these research activities with your students. Once you or your students have an inspiration or topic, you will need to find out more about it. Gather as much information as possible about the topic. The result will be richer if you have more information and possibilities from which to choose. Depending on the grade level with which you are working, you or your students become the information gatherers. Whether information is being gathered for a dance or for a report, the process is the same. You and your students can conduct research using a variety of methods, such as interviewing, thinking as a group, observing, and traditional information gathering.

Interviewing

Interviewing requires students to find experts on their topics. Everyone is an expert on something! A person does not have to have a PhD to be an expert on a subject. Students can rely on family members, community members, and professionals as experts. Students can work in small groups to select people to interview; formulate questions to be asked; and record the responses on audiotape, on videotape, in writing, or in any combination of these choices. Interviews can be conducted by e-mail, over the phone, or in person. Students should learn the proper etiquette involved in conducting an interview, such as contacting the experts beforehand, setting up appointments, getting release forms signed, sending the experts thank-you notes for their time, providing copies of any printed materials, and inviting them to the final exhibition.

Thinking As a Group

This is actually a form of interviewing because it involves gathering knowledge from yourself and others on a specific topic. For example, this type of research can be as simple as looking at photos of birds in flight and then coming up with descriptive words or phrases (see table 2.1). One way of thinking as a group is through "chalk talk," a silent method involving writing the topic

Table 2.1 Flight Inspiration Activity As It Relates to Tasks of Choreographic Process (Grades K to 4)

Task	Inspiration activity
Concept task	Inspiration activity: Flight (grades K to 4) Clue: Come fly with me! Topic or source of inspiration: Observing birds flying
Investigation task (observe, come up with ideas)	Instructions: 1. Look at photos or video clips of birds flying. **2. Come up with a list of words describing the various aspects of flight.**
Exploration task (categories)	3. Sort words that are similar in meaning into categories. (An example of a category for the inspiration of a track meet might be types of races; another might be events in which you throw something.) 4. Choose 4 or 5 words from your favorite category. 5. Create a movement signature (an identifying movement or short series of movements) for each of the words. 6. Combine all your movement signatures into one movement phrase. Your movement will look like a bird in flight.
	You are creating a simple movement phrase. A movement phrase is a dance sentence.

on a blackboard or large sheet of paper. Anyone can write down anything that comes to mind concerning the topic. A second way of thinking as a group involves calling out responses that come to mind over a limited time. During this time a recorder writes down all the responses. With younger children you can keep track on a flip chart or board. It is best to limit the "group think" to 10 minutes and then allow time for review. Remind students that all responses are valid and should not be judged at this time.

Observing

Another effective method of gathering research may be observing your inspiration or topic. Perhaps your inspiration is basketball. Observing practice sessions and games then would be a legitimate

Thinking as a group is an effective research method.

research method. Observing is more than just looking at something. It includes all the other senses: taste, touch, hearing, and smell. To be a good observer you must first clear your mind of all thoughts. To observe, you must pay attention to what you see, to what you hear, and to how something feels to the touch. Sometimes even taste can give you valuable information. (Use common sense about what you put into your mouth.) Observation requires patience and careful recording of the details. It also means that an impartial observer needs to know the difference between recording actual details and recording personal impressions. For instance, when observing a trash truck rumbling down the street, we see trash flying out of the back of the truck and floating to the ground. That is an actual detail. If a personal impression is added, the observer might say that the driver didn't seem to care.

Traditional Information Gathering

Traditional information gathering is not so traditional anymore. It still involves going to an information resource and taking notes. Resources for traditional research are museums, films and videos, field trips, interviews, lectures, libraries, artwork, drawings, photos, surveys, maps, and yellow pages. However, technology has changed the way we receive and record information. Today we do not always have to rely on paper and pencil to record our notes. CD-ROMs, Internet, videotape recordings, DVDs, and audio recorders all make the job of traditional information gathering easier. Forms 2.1 through 2.4, which appear on the CD-ROM, can aid students in their investigation of a topic.

Using the Investigation Task Worksheets and Handouts

The purpose of the worksheets and handouts for the investigation task is to help students in the job of researching the inspirations or topics. These documents break down into smaller steps the sometimes-overwhelming task of researching. You can use the student handouts and worksheets if you are creating a movement activity for students or if you are choreographing your own movement phrase from a concept or topic. Both you and the students can use the worksheets as they are. If necessary, younger students can dictate their responses to you or you can directly teach researched information to them after you have done the research.

There are four student worksheets and handouts for chapter 2.

- Form 2.1, Research Worksheet, starts the search for information by helping to identify what you and your students want to know about the inspiration or topic. If you and your students prefer, you can use a KWL chart in place of this worksheet. A KWL chart has three columns with the following headings: K— What do I know about the topic?, W—What do I want to know?, and L—What do I want to learn and how will I find this information?

Form 2.1   Student Worksheet—Investigation Task: Research Worksheet

Name _____ Class _____ Date _____

Your inspiration is _____

Write at least five questions or pieces of information that you want to know about your inspiration or topic.

1. _____
2. _____
3. _____
4. _____
5. _____

You can research topics by using a variety of methods; interviewing, thinking as a group, observing, and traditional information gathering. Write five specific resources (places to look for information) for answers to your questions. (Refer to form 2.2 for a list of research resources.)

1. _____
2. _____
3. _____
4. _____
5. _____

Form 2.1 Student Worksheet—Investigation Task: Research Worksheet from *Dance About Anything* by M. Sprague, H. Scheff, and S. McGreevy-Nichols, 2006, Champaign, IL: Human Kinetics.

- Form 2.2, List of Research Resources, gives ideas for where one can gather information.

Form 2.2 **Student Handout—Investigation Task: List of Research Resources**

- Visit museums
- Look at films, videos, and DVDs
- Interview an expert
- Go on a field trip
- Use Internet or CD-ROMs
- Attend a lecture on your subject
- Go to a library to look up books, encyclopedias, reference material, newspapers, and periodicals
- Look at artwork, drawings, and photographs
- Take a survey
- Look at maps
- Look in the yellow pages

Form 2.2 Student Handout—Investigation Task: List of Research Resources from *Dance About Anything* by M. Sprague, H. Scheff, and S. McGreevy-Nichols, 2006, Champaign, IL: Human Kinetics.

- Form 2.3, Sources and Notes, provides a place to write notes and bibliographic information for sources.

Form 2.3 **Student Worksheet—Investigation Task: Sources and Notes**

Name _____ Class _____ Date _____

Instructions
Use one sheet for each research source. The source of information is

Important information gathered (please list page numbers for each note):

Proper citation for source (refer to form 2.4, Bibliography Reference Sheet):

Rubric

(+): More than 1 type of research resource is used. Four to six resources are used. Notes contain relevant and important information on the inspiration or topic. Proper citation is used.

(✓): Two or three resources are used. Notes contain relevant information on the inspiration or topic. Proper citation is used.

(–): Fewer than 2 resources are used, and/or there are few notes, and/or the information is not helpful or relevant to the inspiration or topic.

Form 2.3 Student Worksheet—Investigation Task: Sources and Notes from *Dance About Anything* by M. Sprague, H. Scheff, and S. McGreevy-Nichols, 2006, Champaign, IL: Human Kinetics.

- Form 2.4, Bibliography Reference Sheet, gives information on writing a correctly formatted bibliography using American Psychological Association (APA) style.

Form 2.4   Student Handout—Investigation Task: Bibliography Reference Sheet

In a bibliography entry, list each author's or editor's last name first. Organize your sources alphabetically by the author's name, according to the first letter of each entry (even when no author is given). Finally, you must use double spaces and use a reverse indent for sources that run more than one line, as shown in the following examples.

Article on the World Wide Web

Scheff, H., & Sprague, M. (2005, August). *Dance as a cultural research tool.* Electronic paper from Dance Art-i-techts. Retrieved September 30, 2005, from www.danceart-i-techts.com.

Book

Scheff, H., Sprague, M., & McGreevy-Nichols, S. (2005). *Experiencing dance: From student to dance artist.* Champaign, IL: Human Kinetics.

Unknown Author

Merriam-Webster's collegiate dictionary (10th ed.). (1993). Springfield, MA: Merriam-Webster.

Article in Newspaper

Breton, T. (2005, June 17). Operation plunder dome: Cianci's sentence unchanged. *The Providence Journal,* pp. A1, A13.

Encyclopedia (With or Without Bylines)

Bergmann, P.G. (1993). Relativity. In *The new encyclopaedia Britannica* (Vol. 26, pp. 501-508). Chicago: Encyclopaedia Britannica.

Relativity. (1993). In *The new encyclopaedia Britannica* (Vol. 26, pp. 501-508). Chicago: Encyclopaedia Britannica.

Personal Interview

Not necessary in a bibliography. Place in running text only; here is an example: M.J. Sprague (personal communication, June 21, 2005).

Television and Radio

McGreevy-Nichols, S. (Executive Producer). (2007, October 11). *Earthquake in L.A.* [Television broadcast]. Los Angeles: Major Network.

E-Mail Messages

Not necessary in a bibliography. Place in running text only; here is an example: M.J. Sprague (personal communication, June 21, 2005).

Form 2.4 Student Handout—Investigation Task: Bibliography Reference Sheet from *Dance About Anything* by M. Sprague, H. Scheff, and S. McGreevy-Nichols, 2006, Champaign, IL: Human Kinetics. From American Psychological Association (2001). *Publication Manual of the American Psychological Association* (5th ed.). Washington, DC: American Psychological Association.

We hope these worksheets and handouts help you enjoy being information detectives. All these documents are on the CD-ROM in reproducible form.

Chapter 3

Exploration Task: Identifying Important Aspects of the Topic

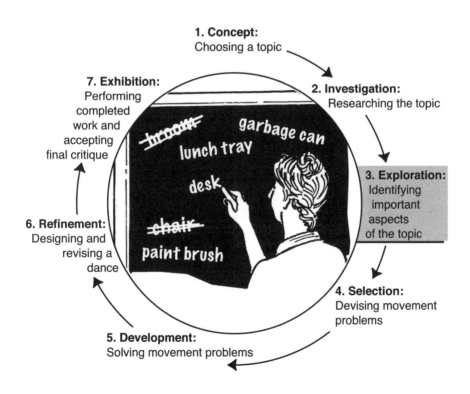

1. **Concept:**
   Choosing a topic

7. **Exhibition:**
   Performing
   completed
   work and
   accepting
   final critique

2. **Investigation:**
   Researching the topic

3. **Exploration:**
   Identifying
   important
   aspects
   of the topic

6. **Refinement:**
   Designing and
   revising a
   dance

4. **Selection:**
   Devising movement
   problems

5. **Development:**
   Solving movement problems

(written on board) ~~broom~~ garbage can lunch tray desk ~~chair~~ paint brush

After gathering information through various methods of research, it is now time to narrow the focus. This is part of the creative and choreographic processes, too. Narrow the focus to make the task of creating something new manageable. This step also affords students the opportunity to pull out specific information from the research and "try it on for size" by organizing very specific aspects from the research and exploring that aspect through movement. Students are able to explore movement options before deciding on the focus of the final product.

Students can approach this task in several ways. To begin this task, students can discuss the following questions: What are the important aspects of the topic? What aspects are most intriguing? What are some images or messages that could be useful when creating the dance? Other methods of approaching this task include developing categories from the research specific to the topic; identifying and selecting pertinent text from the research; and exploring the different aspects using **movement prompts.** *Note:* As a result of any of these types of explorations, it may become apparent that you have enough researched material with which to work. If this is the case, then you and your students can go on to design a dance or other student work. It may also become apparent that more research needs to be done.

Developing Categories

Categories can be used for identifying important aspects of a topic. You and your students should look at all the research and sort it into categories of similar ideas. In the Flight Inspiration Activity, instruction 3 asks the students to place their suggested words into categories of similar ideas (see table 3.1). For instance, some students may organize words by using descriptive words (outspread wings, light as a feather, rudderlike tails, hollow bones) or by using action words (soaring, gliding, dive-bombing, and floating).

These categories then become a source for **movement phrases.** Movement phrases can be thought of as sentences composed of movement. Students are now ready to create movement based on the words in each category. Working with the categories will enable anyone to more easily produce movement that fits together quite naturally.

Table 3.1 Flight Inspiration Activity As It Relates to Tasks of Choreographic Process (Grades K to 4)

Task	Inspiration activity
Concept task	Inspiration activity: Flight (grades K to 4) Clue: Come fly with me! Topic or source of inspiration: Observing birds flying
Investigation task (observe, come up with ideas)	Instructions: 1. Look at photos or video clips of birds flying. 2. Come up with a list of words describing the various aspects of flight.
Exploration task (categories)	**3. Sort words that are similar in meaning into categories. (An example of a category for the inspiration of a track meet might be types of races; another might be events in which you throw something.)** 4. Choose 4 or 5 words from your favorite category. 5. Create a movement signature (an identifying movement or short series of movements) for each of the words. 6. Combine all your movement signatures into one movement phrase. Your movement will look like a bird in flight.
	You are creating a simple movement phrase. A movement phrase is a dance sentence.

Selecting Text

Students or teachers can select important excerpts of text from the collection of written research. For example, the Flight Inspiration Activity for grades 9 to 12 (table 3.4 on page 43) focuses on Sir Isaac Newton's three laws of motion. Out of all the great quantities of information on the topic of flight, this piece could serve as an important aspect because it is fundamental to the physics of flight.

After you or your students select important excerpts from the written research, you can facilitate an open general discussion of the text. Using the Flight Inspiration Activity for grades 5 to 8 (see table 3.3 on page 42), a discussion question could be "What part of the text makes the biggest impression?" A student might answer, "I liked the explanation of how lift, weight, thrust, and drag make the giant 747 airliners fly." You can pool and record the students' collective knowledge **(prior knowledge)** about the topic by asking the questions "What part of the text can you relate to personally?" and "What do you already know about the topic?" A student might answer, "I remember the vacation when I got to go on a hang glider. I was soaring through the air like a bird! It must have been the lift." Students can make connections between the newly researched material and other topics by answering the question "What other topics, issues, or ideas come to mind as a result of reading this material?" A student could come up with the following connecting questions: "How does flight differ at different altitudes? What changes need to be made in the design of the flying apparatus?" Students can connect emotionally to the topic by considering the question "What feelings are evoked by reading this material?" A student may respond by saying, "When life seems tough, I would love to be able to soar like an eagle over all my problems."

Allowing ample time for discussion is critical to this process. This discussion time will enhance the richness of the final product. Use thinking as a group, general group discussions, and comments on questions to focus the work. These strategies bring out the aspects and images that you want to get across to the audience. You and your students are now ready to develop movement for dances.

Using Movement Prompts

You and your students can choose important aspects of a topic by using movement prompts. Movement prompts are similar to writing prompts in that they inspire students to explore different types of movement. A movement prompt encourages students to explore an idea through improvised movement, just as a writing prompt can be used to encourage students to write freely. For example, instruction 5 of the Flight Inspiration Activity for grades K to 4 (see table 3.2 on page 41) asks students to create a **movement signature** (an identifying movement or short series of movements) for each of the words in one or more categories. If students have come up with words such as *soaring, gliding, dive-bombing, flapping,* and *floating,* one can easily imagine the movement signatures students could create from this movement prompt.

A simple way to make movement prompts is to identify action or descriptive words in the research material or words that come to mind because of the material. Students or teachers can choose different images, events, messages, and words from their research. These images, events, messages, and words can then be used to create movement prompts. The movement prompts, in turn, are used to generate movement. Some movement prompts will more easily lend themselves to movement. These will be richer sources than others for interesting movement.

Also, students naturally will prefer to explore some movement ideas

Exploration through movement can help students identify important aspects of the topic.

over others. These more successful movement prompts can help teachers and students in the exploration and identification of important aspects of the topic (i.e., the exploration task).

Using the Exploration Task Worksheets and Handouts

The purpose of the worksheets and handouts for the exploration task is to help you and your students narrow the focus to identify the important aspects of the topic. There is a worksheet for each of the following ways of completing the exploration task:

- Developing categories
- Selecting text
- Using movement prompts

The worksheets and handouts help you and your students explore different movements while narrowing the important aspects of the topic. A by-product of the exploration task will be innovative movement phrases.

Both you and most of the students can use the worksheets as they are. Younger students can dictate their responses to you. You can use the responses to help them explore the topic through movement. There are six worksheets and one handout on the CD-ROM that relate to this chapter. You and your students can choose which of the worksheets you will use. Remember that each worksheet is designed to take you through one of the ways to complete the exploration task.

- The first student worksheet is form 3.1, Using Visualization to Select Text for Movement.

Form 3.1   **Student Worksheet—Exploration Task: Using Visualization to Select Text for Movement**

Name _____ Class _____ Date _____

Instructions

Read through your collected research material. As you read, identify and describe specific images that you visualize (seeing pictures in your mind as you read words and sentences). Focus on one image (one word or sentence) at a time rather than combining many images (a paragraph or entire text). Use a separate worksheet for each image.

1. Describe or draw the image that you visualized in your mind.

2. List the words from the text that describe the image.

3. List the movement ideas that you wish to try when creating a "moving image" for the audience. (A moving image is an idea, topic, concept, emotion, or storyline communicated through movement.)

Form 3.1 Student Worksheet—Exploration Task: Using Visualization to Select Text for Movement from *Dance About Anything* by M. Sprague, H. Scheff, and S. McGreevy-Nichols, 2006, Champaign, IL: Human Kinetics.

- The second worksheet is form 3.2, Images, Events, Messages, and Words Taken From Research for Movement Prompts. This helps the students identify sources for movement prompts.

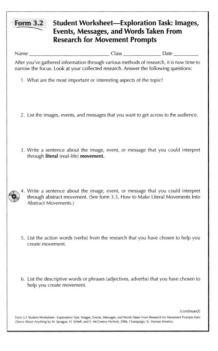

Form 3.2   Student Worksheet—Exploration Task: Images, Events, Messages, and Words Taken From Research for Movement Prompts

Name _____ Class _____ Date _____

After you've gathered information through various methods of research, it is now time to narrow the focus. Look at your collected research. Answer the following questions:

1. What are the most important or interesting aspects of the topic?

2. List the images, events, and messages that you want to get across to the audience.

3. Write a sentence about the image, event, or message that you could interpret through **literal** (real-life) **movement.**

4. Write a sentence about the image, event, or message that you could interpret through abstract movement. (See form 3.3, How to Make Literal Movements Into Abstract Movements.)

5. List the action words (verbs) from the research that you have chosen to help you create movement.

6. List the descriptive words or phrases (adjectives, adverbs) that you have chosen to help you create movement.

(continued)

Form 3.2 Student Worksheet—Exploration Task: Images, Events, Messages, and Words Taken From Research for Movement Prompts from *Dance About Anything* by M. Sprague, H. Scheff, and S. McGreevy-Nichols, 2006, Champaign, IL: Human Kinetics.

- Form 3.3, How to Make Literal Movements Into Abstract Movements, will help students complete the previous document.

Form 3.3   Student Handout—How to Make Literal Movements Into Abstract Movements

The following are some ways to help you make literal movements into abstract movements. The example we use is the literal movement of a handshake.

- Change the rhythm. For example, make the rhythm of the handshake uneven; instead of going only up and down, shake up, up, down.
- Change or vary the speed. For example, shake hands very slowly and then extremely fast.
- Change or vary the size of the movement. For example, make the handshake so small that you can barely see it or so large that you have to move from a high level to a low level.
- Repeat the movement over and over. For example, repeat the movement until it loses its significance as a gesture and becomes simply a movement.
- Use the same movement with a different body part. For example, do the handshake movement with your elbow, foot, or head.
- Do the opposite action and combine it with the original movement. For example, instead of facing the person you are greeting, turn away as if to ignore the other person.
- Make a new, unrelated movement and mix it with the original movement. For example, spin on your toes and connect it with a handshake.
- Interrupt or have the movement take a detour to augment the original movement. For example, begin to shake hands, then use a **locomotor movement** (movement that travels) to travel away, and finally return to finish the handshake.
- Let the movement grow and change. For example, repeat the handshake until it starts to change, and follow it wherever it might lead.

Form 3.3 Student Handout—How to Make Literal Movements Into Abstract Movements from *Dance About Anything* by M. Scheff, and S. McGreevy-Nichols, 2006, Champaign, IL: Human Kinetics. Reprinted, by permission, from S. McGreevy-Nichols, H. Scheff, and M. Sprague, 2001, *Building More Dances* (Champaign, IL: Human Kinetics), 20.

Reprinted, by permission, from S. McGreevy-Nichols, H. Scheff, and M. Sprague, 2001, *Building more dances* (Champaign, IL: Human Kinetics), 20.

- There are two worksheets for developing categories. The first, Idea and Word Sort for Categories (form 3.4), is designed for students to use words and icons; the second, Developing Categories (form 3.5), is for developing categories by just using words.

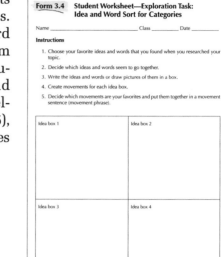

Form 3.4 **Student Worksheet—Exploration Task: Idea and Word Sort for Categories**

Name _____ Class _____ Date _____

Instructions

1. Choose your favorite ideas and words that you found when you researched your topic.
2. Decide which ideas and words seem to go together.
3. Write the ideas and words or draw pictures of them in a box.
4. Create movements for each idea box.
5. Decide which movements are your favorites and put them together in a movement sentence (movement phrase).

Idea box 1	Idea box 2
Idea box 3	Idea box 4

Form 3.4 Student Worksheet—Exploration Task: Idea and Word Sort for Categories from *Dance About Anything* by M. Sprague, H. Scheff, and S. McGreevy-Nichols, 2006, Champaign, IL: Human Kinetics.

Form 3.5 **Student Worksheet—Exploration Task: Developing Categories**

Name _____ Class _____ Date _____

Categories can be used for identifying aspects of a topic. Look at all the research for your topic and sort it into categories. These categories then become a source for movement phrases. Movement phrases can be thought of as sentences composed of movement. You are now ready to create movement based on the words in each category.

1. Look through all the research that you found on your topic or idea.
2. Sort the images, events, messages, and words into categories of similar ideas. Write the category lists here.

3. Create movements for each word and organize them into movement phrases for each category.

Rubric

(+): There are enough images, events, messages, and words to be sorted into 5 or 6 like categories, and a movement phrase is made for each of the categories.

(✓): There are enough images, events, messages, and words to be sorted into 3 or 4 like categories, and a movement phrase is made for each of the categories.

(–): There are 2 or fewer categories, or the categories are not clearly organized, or there are fewer than 3 movement phrases made.

Form 3.5 Student Worksheet—Exploration Task: Developing Categories from *Dance About Anything* by M. Sprague, H. Scheff, and S. McGreevy-Nichols, 2006, Champaign, IL: Human Kinetics.

- Form 3.6, Using Text to Make Movement, allows students to select texts from their research that they think they can represent through movement.

Form 3.6 Student Worksheet—Exploration Task: Using Text to Make Movement

Name _____ Class _____ Date _____

1. From your research resources, choose the most important or interesting texts that you think you can represent through movement. These are the images, events, and messages that you will communicate to the audience. List these texts here.

2. Looking back over the selected text, for each image, event, or message, write down words that will help you develop movements for the image, event, or message that you are trying to communicate to the audience.

   a. The movement phrase can represent _____.
      The following are words and phrases from the text that can help create the movement phrase:
      - _____
      - _____
      - _____
      - _____
      - _____

   b. The movement phrase can represent _____
      _____. The following are words and phrases from the text that can help create the movement phrase:
      - _____
      - _____
      - _____
      - _____
      - _____

(continued)

Form 3.6 Student Worksheet—Exploration Task: Using Text to Make Movement from *Dance About Anything* by M. Sprague, H. Scheff, and S. McGreevy-Nichols, 2006, Champaign, IL: Human Kinetics.

- Form 3.7, Movement Prompts, takes students through the process of developing and dancing to their own movement prompts. Again, these reproducible forms can be found on the CD-ROM.

Form 3.7 Student Worksheet—Exploration Task: Movement Prompts

Name _____ Class _____ Date _____

1. Identify action and descriptive words that are in the research material or that come to mind because of the material. For example, if the topic is the flight of birds, the following action words could be identified: soaring, gliding, dive-bombing, flapping, and floating. Examples of descriptive words or phrases that could be identified are outspread wings, light as a feather, hollow bones, and rudderlike tail.

   Write the action words based on your research material here.

   Write the descriptive words or phrases based on your research materials here.

2. Ask yourself questions that you can answer in movement. Write the questions here.

3. Move and explore your movement prompts. Write the ones that inspire the most interesting movement here. This will show you which aspects of the topic should be chosen.

4. Write your favorite movement prompts here. If possible, have your movement phrases videotaped.

Rubric

(+): Student has compiled a list of 7 or more movement prompts; has explored (danced) at least 5 of them; and has selected their 3 best movement prompts.

(✓): Student has compiled a list of at least 5 movement prompts and has explored (danced) at least 3 of them.

(−): Student has made 4 or fewer movement prompts and/or has explored (danced) 2 or fewer and/or the movement prompts and movements need much revision.

Form 3.7 Student Worksheet—Exploration Task: Movement Prompts from *Dance About Anything* by M. Sprague, H. Scheff, and S. McGreevy-Nichols, 2006, Champaign, IL: Human Kinetics.

Using the Inspiration Activity Cards

The Inspiration Activity Cards on the CD-ROM (forms 3.8 to 3.15) are designed for the students to use so that they can experience the first three tasks. You only need to be a facilitator when you use these cards as part of your lessons. Each Inspiration Activity Card is on one page with a fold line in the middle of the page so that you can print the cards from the CD-ROM and make the cards with the inspiration text on one side and the instructions on the other side.

On the front side of the card, the clue is the tool to get the students interested in participating in the investigation and exploration of the topic. On the flip side of the card, the topic is the big idea, the concept. It is the source of your inspiration. The clue then is repeated. The topic or source of inspiration is a more specific aspect of the concept. The instructions on the card give step-by-step guidance to your students. The inspiration note at the bottom of each card explains that a movement phrase is like a dance sentence. All you need to do is have the students pick an Inspiration Activity Card and the students can proceed from there.

Included on the CD-ROM is a detailed Inspiration Activity Card illustrating what to include in each section (form 3.16). Also included on the CD-ROM is a blank Inspiration Activity Card (form 3.17). Using this format, you can create your own inspiration activities. Your students, at any grade level, will have a great time creating these cards, as well. The cards use the first three tasks of the choreographic process. Feel free to have fun and play.

Summary of Part I

In part I you have been introduced to the first three tasks of the choreographic process. In the concept task (choosing a topic), you have seen how the topic or concept is the *what* that you are trying to investigate, explore, or communicate through movement. Whether the topic is a single word or a complex theme, it is your inspiration for creating. There is no right or wrong answer or procedure when following an inspiration. The investigation task (researching the topic) provides you and your students the opportunity to gather a variety of information on the topic. You and your students can obtain this information using a number of methods that are discussed in part I: interviewing, thinking as a group, observing, and traditional information gathering. Finally, in the exploration task (identifying important aspects of the topic), learners experiment with content, ideas, and movement to narrow the focus of the topic.

Table 3.2 Flight Inspiration Activity As It Relates to Tasks of Choreographic Process (Grades K to 4)

Task	Inspiration activity
Concept task	Inspiration activity: Flight (grades K to 4) Clue: Come fly with me! Topic or source of inspiration: Observing birds flying
Investigation task (observe, come up with ideas)	Instructions: 1. Look at photos or video clips of birds flying. 2. Come up with a list of words describing the various aspects of flight.
Exploration task (categories)	3. Sort words that are similar in meaning into categories. (An example of a category for the inspiration of a track meet might be types of races; another might be events in which you throw something.) 4. Choose 4 or 5 words from your favorite category. 5. Create a movement signature (an identifying movement or short series of movements) for each of the words. 6. Combine all your movement signatures into one movement phrase. Your movement will look like a bird in flight.
	You are creating a simple movement phrase. A movement phrase is a dance sentence.

Table 3.3   Flight Inspiration Activity As It Relates to Tasks of Choreographic Process (Grades 5 to 8)

Task	Inspiration activity
Concept task	Inspiration activity: Flight (grades 5 to 8) Clue: May the force be with you Topic or source of inspiration: The four forces of flight
Investigation task (research)	Instructions: 1. Research the four words relating to the topic of flight. These words are *lift, weight, propulsion,* and *drag.*
Exploration task (movement prompt)	2. Create a moving definition for each of the four words, based on the definition of each of the words. (A moving definition is movement that expresses the meaning of a word.) 3. Combine the four moving definitions in any order you wish to make a larger moving definition of the word *flight.*
	You are creating a simple movement phrase. A movement phrase is a dance sentence.

Table 3.4　Flight Inspiration Activity As It Relates to Tasks of Choreographic Process (Grades 9 to 12)

Task	Inspiration activity
Concept task	Inspiration activity: Flight (grades 9 to 12) Clue: It's the law! Topic or source of inspiration: Flight and Newton's laws of motion
Investigation task (research)	Instructions: 1. Read Sir Isaac Newton's three laws of motion (Dynamic Flight, 1999-2004): I. **Inertia:** A body at rest will remain at rest, and a body in motion will remain in motion at the same speed and direction until affected by some external force. Nothing starts or stops without an outside force to bring about or prevent motion. Hence, the force with which a body offers resistance to change is called the force of inertia. II. **Acceleration:** The force required to produce a change in motion of a body is directly proportional to its mass and the rate of change in its velocity. Acceleration refers to either an increase or a decrease in velocity, although deceleration is commonly used to indicate a decrease. III. **Action and reaction:** For every action there is an equal and opposite reaction. If an interaction occurs between two bodies, equal forces in opposite directions will be imparted to each body. 2. Working in small groups, experiment with marbles or toy cars to test the three laws of motion.
Exploration task (movement prompt)	3. In your groups, create movement phrases demonstrating the meaning for each of the three laws of motion. To do this, translate the movement you saw in the experiment into dance movement. 4. Have someone read out loud each law while your group dances the movement phrase for that law.
💡	You are creating a simple movement phrase. A movement phrase is a dance sentence.

Part II

Dance Designing
From Solving Movement Problems to Exhibition

Dance About Anything lets you and your students decide what you should dance about. Part II takes you through the last four tasks in the choreographic process. In chapter 4, Selection Task, you devise movement problems from your selected aspects of the topics. Chapter 5, Development and Refinement Tasks, explores how to solve those movement problems and helps you take the solutions, or movement phrases, and design and refine a dance. Chapter 6, Exhibition Task, brings the whole creative process to a climax with the exhibition task and the accepting of a final critique.

At the end of part II (pp. 76-82) you will find copies of the Flight Dance Designing Activities. They are in table format (tables 6.1, 6.2, and 6.3), highlighting the seven tasks of the cognitive processes.

Chapter 4

Selection Task: Devising Movement Problems

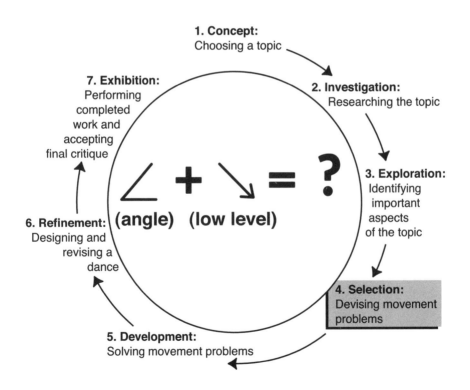

1. **Concept:**
Choosing a topic

2. **Investigation:**
Researching the topic

3. **Exploration:**
Identifying
important
aspects
of the topic

4. **Selection:**
Devising movement
problems

5. **Development:**
Solving movement problems

6. **Refinement:**
Designing and
revising a
dance

7. **Exhibition:**
Performing
completed
work and
accepting
final critique

∠ + ↘ = **?**
(angle)   **(low level)**

A part of creative thinking is the ability to recognize a problem that already exists or, in order to organize and focus your work, actually design a new problem. As we work through the creative process, during the selection task we ask questions, identify existing problems, invent new problems to solve, and map out methods for solving the problems. Designing movement problems (selection task) and solving movement problems (development task) are basic and inherent parts of the choreographic process. Questions to be asked or problems to be solved must engage a choreographer's interest even before one movement is created. These guiding thoughts, questions, or problems frame the entire dance before, during, and after its creation. Teaching students how to design movement problems allows them to use the new knowledge that they have gained during the research phase; ultimately, this approach will help them retain that knowledge. (Refer to the section titled Advocacy: Supporting Educational Theory in the introduction.)

Movement Problems Defined

A movement problem is a puzzle that, when solved, will produce original movement phrases. Movement problems are similar to math word problems and word and logic puzzles. Consider the following math word problem: Jenny bought three pairs of shoes. Two of the pairs of shoes cost $21.15 each. The other pair cost $14.50. How much did the shoes cost in all? In this problem, certain information is given and questions are asked. Sometimes hints or suggestions are given in the problem, which help us to discover the method or procedure to be used to come up with a solution. Movement problems also have all of these characteristics, but their solutions produce movement phrases. Movement phrases can then be manipulated and organized to create entire dances.

Through the use of student-produced movement problems, we have found that students develop a deeper understanding of the topic of a dance. By creating their own movement problems, students use critical-thinking skills. Students are pleasantly surprised by the beautiful and original movement that other students generate from their movement problems. Students are also able to transfer what they learn from writing movement problems to taking apart a math problem, a prerequisite for solving written math problems. The remainder of this chapter walks you through the steps and gives you the tools to help your students create movement problems. It will guide you in choosing ideas for use in movement problems; choosing movement and dance ideas for movement problems; choosing the procedure for use in movement problems; writing the movement problems; and using the selection task worksheets and handouts.

Choosing Ideas for Use in Movement Problems

Previously in the exploration task, you asked students guiding questions about what images, events, feelings, or ideas were foremost in their minds as they considered the information that they had accumulated during their research. From this kind of focusing discussion, you and your students can come up with not only the main idea, theme, or image of the dance but also other smaller ideas or bits of information gleaned from the research. These large and small ideas are identified in the movement problem and should be visible in the **movement solution** (phrase). Use of information from the research provides the working material or information to be used in the design of the movement problem.

For instance, in the Flight Dance Designing Activity (Grades K to 4, table 6.1 on page 75), the main idea for the movement problem is showing how and why birds move in certain ways. Students may decide that the verbs and verb phrases in the reading selection are what they wish to focus on (exploration task). These verbs and verb phrases could be (1) flapping for taking off, turning, landing, and moving quickly from place to place; (2) flapping in a rowing or figure-eight motion; (3) gliding on outstretched wings and between short bursts of flapping and gliding often and gliding very little; and (4) soaring by allowing thermals to carry them. The students could decide that these five types of flying movements would be the smaller ideas that show how and why birds move in special ways.

Choosing Movement and Dance Ideas for Movement Problems

- After identifying the main idea and the smaller ideas that should appear in the movement problem (and later, in the dance), you can then ask the students to choose specific movement and dance ideas (see Dance Ideas List, form 4.1). Choices made from the Dance Ideas List should be based on finding ways of making the main idea and the smaller ideas the most clear. In other words, the choices made should be the best fit. For example, if a student is trying to develop the small idea of flapping for taking off, leaps might be a better choice for a locomotor movement than walking because of the acceleration involved in taking off.

Form 4.1 **Student Worksheet—Selection Task: Dance Ideas List**

Name _____ Class _____ Date _____

Instructions
Choose the dance ideas that express the idea, theme, or image.

Movement Skills
[ ] balance [ ] falls and recoveries [ ] isolations [ ] weight shifts

Locomotor Movements
[ ] walk [ ] hop [ ] jump [ ] leap [ ] assemblé (jump from one foot to two feet)
[ ] sissonne (jump from two feet to one foot) [ ] slide [ ] skip [ ] gallop

Nonlocomotor Movements
[ ] bend [ ] twist [ ] stretch

Movement Qualities
[ ] smooth [ ] swing [ ] percussive [ ] collapse [ ] vibratory

Movement Elements (Laban Efforts)
Weight: [ ] strength [ ] lightness
Time: [ ] sudden [ ] sustained
Space: [ ] direct [ ] indirect
Flow: [ ] bound [ ] free

Effort Elements (Laban Effort Actions)
[ ] dab [ ] punch [ ] float [ ] glide [ ] wring [ ] press [ ] flick [ ] slash

Choreographic Structures
[ ] canon [ ] collage [ ] AB [ ] accumulation [ ] ABA [ ] call and response [ ] rondo
[ ] chance dance [ ] theme and variations [ ] beginning, middle, and end
[ ] narrative (sequential time line of events) [ ] ground bass

Choreographic Processes
[ ] transition [ ] contrast [ ] complementary [ ] copying

Choreographic Elements
Organizing Dancers in the Dance
[ ] solo [ ] duet [ ] trio [ ] ensemble [ ] facings of dancers [ ] formations [ ] symmetrical shapes and formations [ ] asymmetrical shapes and formations [ ] partnering and weight sharing

(continued)

Form 4.1 Student Worksheet—Selection Task: Dance Ideas List from *Dance About Anything* by M. Sprague, H. Scheff, and S. McGreevy-Nichols, 2006, Champaign, IL: Human Kinetics. Adapted, by permission, from H. Scheff, M. Sprague, and S. McGreevy-Nichols, 2005, *Experiencing Dance: From Student to Dance Artist* (Champaign, IL: Human Kinetics), 121-122.

Adapted, by permission, from H. Scheff, M. Sprague, and S. McGreevy-Nichols, 2005, *Experiencing dance: From student to dance artist* (Champaign, IL: Human Kinetics), 121-122.

- Movement and dance ideas can include **movement skills, locomotor** and **nonlocomotor movements, movement qualities, effort elements (Laban efforts;** see *Building More Dances,* McGreevy-Nichols, Scheff, and Sprague, 2001, p. 17), **effort actions (Laban actions) choreographic structures, choreographic processes,** and **choreographic elements.** For definitions of these terms, see the glossary; form 4.2, Choreographic Structures Resource Sheet; and form 4.3, Choreographic

Processes and Elements Resource Sheet. Both of these forms are on the CD-ROM. Identified choices from the Dance Ideas List (form 4.1) will eventually be included in the written movement problem. Other simple ideas, such as how long the finished movement solution (movement phrase or answer to the movement problem) should be, can also be included in the written movement problem.

Form 4.2   Student Handout—Choreographic Structures Resource Sheet

Choreographic Structures

- A **canon**, also known as a round, is two or more movement parts involved in a composition in which the main movement is imitated exactly and completely by the successive movements, but the different parts are staggered. It is the equivalent of singing "Row, Row, Row Your Boat" in staggered parts but using movement in place of the words.
- The **AB** format can be described as A (a dance phrase) and B (a new dance phrase).
- The **ABA** format can be described as A (a dance phrase), B (a new dance phrase), and a return to A (the first dance phrase).
- A **rondo** can be described as ABACADA. The choreographic pattern begins with a main theme (A) followed by another theme or movement material, and the A theme returns after each new movement phrase.
- **Theme and variation** format can be described as a dance phrase or section of a dance with subsequent dance phrases or sections being variations of the original. This would be A, A1, A2, A3.
- The **narrative** choreographic form tells a story or conveys an idea. The sequence of the story determines the structure of the dance.
- **Collage** is a choreographic form that consists of a series of movement phrases that are often unrelated but have been brought together to create a single dance with a beginning, a middle, and an end.
- **Accumulation** is a choreographic form that can be described by the following model: (1), (1, 2), (1, 2, 3), (1, 2, 3, 4), (1, 2, 3, 4, 5). If each number represents a distinct movement or dance phrase, then this structure is constructed by adding on different movement or dance phrases.
- **Call and response** as a choreographic form can be described as conversational: One person moves and the other person's movement responds to (answers) the movement of the initial mover, just as in a tap challenge.
- **Chance dance** is a series of dance phrases performed in a random order. Each time the dance is done, it is in a different order and therefore has a different appearance.
- **Motif and development** is a brief movement phrase that is danced and then developed into a full-blown dance or section of a dance.
- **Suite** uses different tempos and qualities in each of its three or more sections. Usually the first section is a moderate tempo, the second is an adagio (slow tempo), and the last section is an allegro (fast tempo).
- **Beginning, middle, and end** are basic to all the choreographic structures. A dance should have a beginning shape or pose or entrance, a middle consisting of development or exploration of the main idea, and a clear end consisting of a shape or pose or exit.

(continued)

Form 4.2 Student Handout—Choreographic Structures Resource Sheet from *Dance About Anything* by M. Sprague, H. Scheff, and S. McGreevy-Nichols, 2006, Champaign, IL: Human Kinetics. Adapted, by permission, from H. Scheff, M. Sprague, and S. McGreevy-Nichols, 2005, *Experiencing Dance: From Student to Dance Artist* (Champaign, IL: Human Kinetics), 106-107.

Adapted, by permission, from H. Scheff, M. Sprague, and S. McGreevy-Nichols, 2005, *Experiencing dance: From student to dance artist* (Champaign, IL: Human Kinetics), 106-107.

Form 4.3   Student Handout—Choreographic Processes and Elements Resource Sheet

Choreographic Processes

- A **transition** connects one movement or movement phrase to the next movement or movement phrase. For example, if a movement at a low level is followed by a movement at a high level, you can insert a transitional movement at the middle level.
- The choreographic process of **contrast** adds interest through developing opposite shapes, movements, or movement phrases. For example, if you have a shape made of angles, for contrast, you would then make a shape using curves.
- **Complementary** choreographic process involves developing different but related shapes, movements, or movement phrases. For example, if you make a shape out of curves, you make a different shape, but still use curves. It is as though the complementary shapes, movements, or movement phrases are "cousins" to the original shapes, movements, or movement phrases. They are similar, but not precisely the same.
- The choreographic process of **copying** is exactly what the name implies: The choreographer repeats an already-existing shape, movement, or movement phrase at a later time in the dance or in a different space on the stage.

Choreographic Elements

These are elements that organize the dancers in the dance.

- The terms **solo, duet, trio,** and **ensemble** relate to the number of people dancing at one time.
- The **facings** of dancers are the stage directions to which dancers perform their movements.
- **Groupings and formations** indicate where dancers stand in relation to other dancers.
- **Symmetrical shapes and formations** are the same on both sides of a centerline. For example, in a symmetrical formation there would be an equal number of dancers on each side of the centerline of the stage. Both sides of the stage would look the same.
- **Asymmetrical shapes and formations** are different on both sides of a centerline. For example, in an asymmetrical formation there would be an unequal number of dancers on each side of the centerline of the stage. There could be one dancer on one side and four on the other side.
- **Partnering and weight sharing** means guiding, giving, and taking weight from another dancer.

The following are elements that manipulate the movement within a dance.

- **Unison** means that the dancers are all moving at the same time and doing the same movement in the same way.
- **Repetition** means that a movement or movement pattern is repeated.

(continued)

Form 4.3 Student Handout—Choreographic Processes and Elements Resource Sheet from *Dance About Anything* by M. Sprague, H. Scheff, and S. McGreevy-Nichols, 2006, Champaign, IL: Human Kinetics. Adapted, by permission, from H. Scheff, M. Sprague, and S. McGreevy-Nichols, 2005, *Experiencing Dance: From Student to Dance Artist* (Champaign, IL: Human Kinetics), 207, 209, 213.

Adapted, by permission, from H. Scheff, M. Sprague, and S. McGreevy-Nichols, 2005, *Experiencing dance: From student to dance artist* (Champaign, IL: Human Kinetics), 207, 209, 213.

Choosing the Procedure for Use in Movement Problems

After choosing the movement and dance ideas, students can then decide what process should be used to solve the movement problems. Think of the written procedure as the instructions that the dancers need to follow in order to solve the movement problem. Students are usually very adept at this. Some examples of processes include the following:

- Create pantomimed or literal gestures and then abstract them by making them larger or smaller, changing levels, changing facings of dancers, or putting the gestures on other body parts. (For definitions of these terms and more ideas, see form 3.3, How to Make Literal Movements Into Abstract Movements.) In a movement problem, this could be written as "Make the literal movement of washing a dinner plate abstract by putting the circular hand movements into a floor pattern using a locomotor movement and into an air pattern using both arms."

- Create a **movement signature** (simple identifying movements or gestures) for a person, idea, or object; use this signature every time this person, idea, or object is needed in the dance. In a movement problem, this could be written as "Create a movement signature for the word *bird* by making up a shape or a movement that you will use anytime you wish to represent this word in your dance."

- Create shapes related to the main idea or theme and create dance movements to connect them. In a movement problem, this could be written as "Make a shape for each type of bird you would like to represent in your dance. Then use the verbs and verb phrases from your research or text to make movements that are symbolic of that type of bird. Use these movements between the shapes to connect them."

- Set up a situation or relationship between dancers and abstract the resulting literal movements. In a movement problem, this could be written as "Pretend that you are distrustful strangers meeting for the first time, and act out this scenario. Now use form 3.3 (How to Make Literal Movements Into Abstract Movements) to make the movement you used in the scene of strangers meeting more abstract and dancelike."

Students performing their movement solution for an Eastern greeting versus Western greeting movement problem.

The following is a student-created movement problem from a dance in the project Anna and the King. Note the use of a procedure and the list of dance ideas to be used to solve the movement problem.

You are assigned to make up a dance for the section of modernization of Siam carried out by King Mongkut's son. Our research revealed that a railroad system was one of the modern improvements. You are making a movement phrase about the railroad tracks.

1. First, make movements that look as if you are carrying something heavy.
2. Make movement that looks as if you are laying the railroad tracks.

(continued)

(continued)

3. Make a floor pattern that represents the route that the workmen would follow as they assemble the tracks. Use the movement of laying the tracks while you follow the floor pattern.

Use the following dance ideas in your dance sentence: strength, sustained time, and unison steps. Make sure you and your dance partners face each other sometime during the dance.

Writing the Movement Problems

The students should write a final copy of the complete movement problem, which includes the main idea, theme, and image; other ideas from the research; dance ideas; and the process.

- The worksheets titled Designing Movement Problems (form 4.4 for grades K to 4 and form 4.5 for grades 5 to 12 on the CD-ROM) will help the students create their own movement problems.
- When different students start with the same main idea, theme, or image and create more than one movement problem, it is possible to generate more than enough movement for a full dance.
- It will be intriguing how different the movement problems and the movement solutions will be. This is because each student or group of students will bring their own creativity to the activity. When creativity is involved, there is no one right answer.

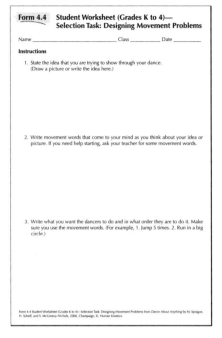

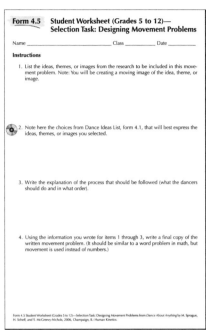

The Dance Designing Activities found in this book are themselves types of movement problems. Here is an example of the first four tasks in the Flight Dance Designing Activity (grades 5 to 8) in table 6.2 (page 78). For clarity, the name of the task used in each numbered instruction is in brackets.

1. Look at the image. Use it as your topic or inspiration for your dance. [Concept task]

2. Research the identified flight concepts and find out how they apply to the flight of birds and to the flight of airplanes. [Investigation task]

3. Compare and contrast the flight abilities of birds and airplanes. To do this, use a two-column list with "compare" in one column and "contrast" in the other or a **Venn diagram.** [Exploration task: categories]

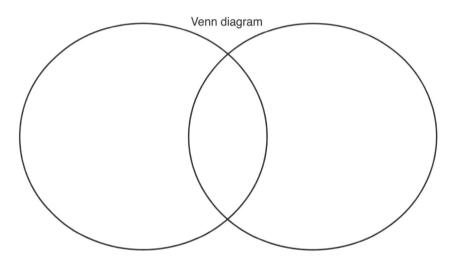

Venn diagram

4. From the Dance Ideas List (form 4.1 on the CD-ROM), choose dance ideas that are best for the different sections of the dance. In other words, choose the dance ideas that best show bird flight and the dance ideas that best show airplane flight. If you want to show the aspects of flight that both birds and airplanes share (from the center of the Venn diagram), choose other dance ideas from the list. [Selection task: movement problem]

5. Use the **AB** choreographic structure if you want to show a simple comparing and contrasting of the flight of birds and airplanes. Use the **rondo** (ABACA) choreographic structure if you want to stress the shared aspects of flight for both birds and airplanes (as A), and use sections B and C for the flight of birds and airplanes, respectively. See form 4.2 on the CD-ROM, Choreographic Structures Resource Sheet, for further information on these two choreographic structures. [Selection task: movement problem]

Using the Selection Task Worksheets and Handouts

The worksheets (form 4.1, Dance Ideas List; form 4.4, Designing Movement Problems [Grades K to 4]; and form 4.5, Designing Movement Problems [Grades 5 to 8]) and the handouts (form 4.2, Choreographic Structures Resource Sheet, and form 4.3, Choreographic Processes and Elements Resource Sheet) are resources written for students and teachers. You may use the handouts as resources so that you can teach the particular information necessary for a specific dance.

In form 4.2, Choreographic Structures Resource Sheet, the patterns used in the definitions can be used for teaching the younger students different organizing choreographic structures. Young students recognize patterns quite easily. For example, teach students about the choreographic structure of **accumulation** by first writing the pattern (1), (1, 2), (1, 2, 3), (1, 2, 3, 4 . . .) for the students to see. Have the students stand in a circle. The first student does a movement that is called (1). All the students repeat this movement and add the second student's movement. This is called (1, 2). The first and second students' movements are repeated, and a third student's movement is added. This is called (1, 2, 3). The pattern is repeated until all students have contributed to the accumulation structure.

Students use form 4.4, Designing Movement Problems, to create their first movement problems. You can help your students with instruction number 2 by giving them a list of vocabulary words appropriate for the ideas to be included in the movement problem. These words can be taken from a research text, the Dance Ideas List (form 4.1), or a group thinking session on the main idea.

Chapter 5

Development and Refinement Tasks: Solving Movement Problems and Designing a Dance

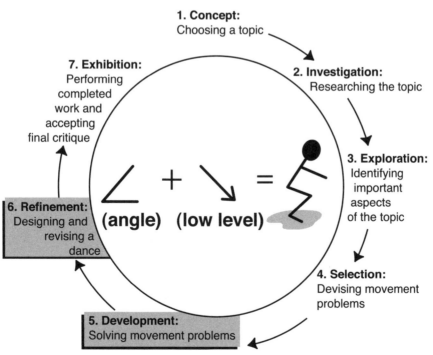

1. Concept: Choosing a topic

2. Investigation: Researching the topic

3. Exploration: Identifying important aspects of the topic

4. Selection: Devising movement problems

5. Development: Solving movement problems

6. Refinement: Designing and revising a dance

7. Exhibition: Performing completed work and accepting final critique

∠ + ↘ = **(angle)** **(low level)**

Many choreographers use dancer-generated movements in their choreography. Designing and solving movement problems allow teachers and students to take advantage of this valid method of choreography. Generally, people look good doing movement that originated from their own imaginations or bodies. By solving the written movement problems, which is the development task, students not only will have developed movement phrases and dance sections that relate to the topic or concept but also will have chosen movement that fits their own physical skills and comfort levels. Once there is a collection of movement phrases or dance sections, there is enough movement to complete the dance. Organizing and arranging this movement and self-evaluating the work to make revisions and improvements on the dance are all part of the refinement task. Dance is a mode of communication and movement problems, and their solutions help the choreographer transform thoughts and ideas into dance.

Development Task: Solving Movement Problems

After the students have determined and written movement problems, they are ready to solve them, thereby creating movement phrases and sections of a dance. At this stage of the process, we suggest that you allow the students to work in small groups. There are two effective methods for deciding which group should solve which movement problem. The first way is to have the students read all the problems and let them choose which ones to solve, which gives them a chance to make critical decisions about the content of the dance. Another more gamelike method is to lay out the written movement problems facedown and let the students randomly choose their problems.

Research material continues to be useful in the development task. If all the students have based their movement problems on the same text, then the groups can go on to solve the problems. If the students have based their movement problems on individual research, it would be helpful if the groups solving the problems had a copy of the particular research text or notes. The students in the solving groups should read the research so that they have some context on which to base their movement solutions. All you (as the teacher) have to do is step back and let the groups follow the instructions in the movement problem. At the end of this activity, you and your students will have enough movement material to make a complete dance.

Small-group work necessitates facilitation skills on your part. While working on the movement solutions, groups of inventive young minds may need you to remind them to stay focused, to clarify a term or instruction, and perhaps to help them value every group member's input. As the students complete the movement solutions, you can then become coach and make observations and suggestions to improve the work. (More details about teaching, facilitating, and coaching are found in chapter 9.)

Refinement Task: Designing and Revising a Dance

The refinement task involves designing the complete dance through the manipulation of the movement material and the revision of the design. In this task, the choreographers (either you or your students or both) use both creative and critical thinking. If your students are making all the decisions about the design of the dance, then they will need direct instruction from you on the types of choreographic structures, processes, and elements (see forms 4.2 and 4.3 on the CD-ROM). The following information and suggestions will be helpful in the design process.

Once the students have solved the movement problems, they can order the different movement solutions or dance sections in a sequence that makes sense to the main topic. They can structure the whole dance based on many different factors. For instance, if the main topic is a **narrative** (a choreographic form that tells a story or conveys an idea), then a time line (a sequence of events) could be the organizing structure. If the main idea is more abstract or general, then perhaps the dance sections can be ordered with the strongest student dance work placed at the beginning and end of the dance. Even the number of students appearing in each dance section can determine the order—a possible organization can build from a solo to a duet to a trio, and so on, to the full ensemble. Students can use choreographic structures, processes, and elements to organize the entire dance as well as the smaller dance phrases. Different movement phrases can occur simultaneously. Choreographic processes can create opposition with the use of opposite-looking movement on stage at the same time (contrast). To add dimension, students can place similar but different (complementary) movement on stage at the same time. Different movement phrases or dance sections can also occur one at a time (sequentially) or perhaps just overlapped (one over the other).

After students decide on the structure and order of the movement phrases or sections, then they can link phrases or sections to create longer dance sequences by using transitional movement (see form 4.3, Choreographic Processes and Elements Resource Sheet). To make transitions, students can create new movement or take movement from the already-created movement phrases. Transitions are helpful in guiding the audience's attention from one section of the dance to another.

This rough draft of the completed dance could be videotaped to be used later for assessment. The students, with your help, can self-evaluate and revise the dance. (Note that when using video, you may need to have a video and photography release form signed by students' parents or guardians. Check with your principal for your school's rule on this matter.) If videotaping is not possible, then use peer and teacher assessments to help the students decide on any revisions. Bringing in an outside observer to give feedback will also help with the revision process. This revision may include any structural reorganization of the dance and rechoreographing of any dance sections that may be unclear. Students may decide whether any movements should be repeated, expanded, or even thrown out. Simply speaking, revision calls for knowing what works in the dance and what doesn't work. What does not work should be changed or deleted. Self-evaluation worksheets have

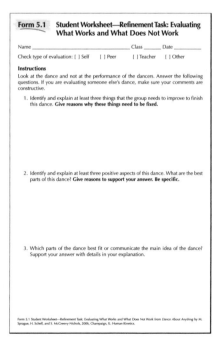

Form 5.1   Student Worksheet—Refinement Task: Evaluating What Works and What Does Not Work

Name _____ Class _____ Date _____

Check type of evaluation: [ ] Self   [ ] Peer   [ ] Teacher   [ ] Other

Instructions
Look at the dance and not at the performance of the dancers. Answer the following questions. If you are evaluating someone else's dance, make sure your comments are constructive.

1. Identify and explain at least three things that the group needs to improve to finish this dance. **Give reasons why these things need to be fixed.**

2. Identify and explain at least three positive aspects of this dance. What are the best parts of this dance? **Give reasons to support your answer. Be specific.**

3. Which parts of the dance best fit or communicate the main idea of the dance? Support your answer with details in your explanation.

Form 5.1 Student Worksheet—Refinement Task: Evaluating What Works and What Does Not Work from *Dance About Anything* by M. Sprague, H. Scheff, and S. McCreevy-Nichols, 2006, Champaign, IL: Human Kinetics.

been included in the student worksheets to help students (and you) with this revision process. See form 5.1, Evaluating What Works and What Does Not Work, and form 5.2, Self-Evaluation of Work. If they wish to give feedback about a dance, peers and teachers may use form 5.1.

To sum up, here is the work done in the development and refinement tasks: The movement problems have been solved, giving us movement phrases or dance sections. This movement material has been manipulated and organized, giving us the rough draft of the complete dance. The dance has been evaluated and necessary revisions have been made, giving us the dance that is now ready for the final rehearsals and the performance. Congratulations to you and your students!

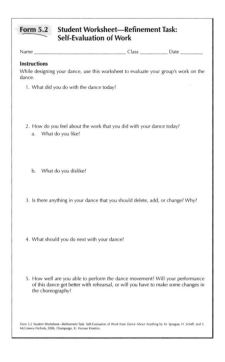

Form 5.2   Student Worksheet—Refinement Task: Self-Evaluation of Work

Name _____ Class _____ Date _____

Instructions
While designing your dance, use this worksheet to evaluate your group's work on the dance.

1. What did you do with the dance today?

2. How do you feel about the work that you did with your dance today?
   a. What do you like?

   b. What do you dislike?

3. Is there anything in your dance that you should delete, add, or change? Why?

4. What should you do next with your dance?

5. How well are you able to perform the dance movement? Will your performance of this dance get better with rehearsal, or will you have to make some changes in the choreography?

Form 5.2 Student Worksheet—Refinement Task: Self-Evaluation of Work from *Dance About Anything* by M. Sprague, H. Scheff, and S. McGreevy-Nichols, 2006, Champaign, IL: Human Kinetics.

Using the Development Task and Refinement Task Worksheets and Handouts

By answering the questions in form 5.3, Reflection on Solving the Movement Problem, students reflect on the process of solving the movement problems and on whether they are satisfied with the movement phrases or dance sections that they and their groups have made. Students can decide whether their movement phrase or dance section fits the topic of the dance and whether it should be included in the completed dance. There is also a question that asks for a critique of the movement problem itself. This student worksheet can be used as a written reflection or as the basis for a teacher-led discussion.

To more fully develop the student-generated movement phrases or dance sections, students (and you if you are the one arranging your students' movement phrases) can use form 5.4, Playing With Your Movement Phrase or Dance Section. Suggestions are given, using choreographic elements and processes, to expand the students' movement material. Students are asked to play around with their movement and decide which elements and processes they wish to include in their movement phrases or dance sections.

Form 5.5, Putting It All Together, helps your students (or you, if you are helping the younger students with this task) make a final structure for the complete dance. Using this worksheet along with form 4.2, Choreographic Structures Resource Sheet, students can include choreographic structures in their dance sections, decide on an order for the different groups' dance sections, and finally, try some structures to organize the entire dance. For example, if everyone especially likes a particular movement phrase (call it A), it could be used to connect all the other groups' dance sections. This structure would then be a rondo form (ABACAD . . .).

Form 5.3 **Student Worksheet—Development Task: Reflection on Solving the Movement Problem**

Name _____ Class _____ Date _____

Instructions

To help you reflect on solving the movement problem, answer the following questions.

1. How did your group choose your movement problem?

2. Were the instructions and information given in the movement problem clear enough for your group to understand and follow? What suggestions for improvement (if any) do you have for the authors of the movement problem?

3. Do you like the movement that your group made? Why or why not?

4. Does this movement fit the topic of the dance? Why or why not?

5. Should this movement be included in the dance? Why or why not?

Form 5.3 Student Worksheet—Development Task: Reflection on Solving the Movement Problem from *Dance About Anything* by M. Sprague, H. Scheff, and S. McGreevy-Nichols, 2006, Champaign, IL: Human Kinetics.

Form 5.4 **Student Worksheet—Refinement Task: Playing With Your Movement Phrase or Dance Section**

Name _____ Class _____ Date _____

Instructions

Using the following choices, arrange and make additions to your movement phrase. To do this, try many different dance ideas. If you need help with the definitions of the dance ideas, ask your teacher or look at the Choreographic Processes and Elements Resource Sheet (form 4.3).

Using Choreographic Elements

1. If the movement problem has not already asked you to do this, you and your group add choreographic elements to organize the dancers in the dance. Using the movement phrases, play with the following elements:
   ___ The number of dancers dancing at one time
   ___ The way the dancers face
   ___ Different formations (groupings)
   ___ Add partnering (optional)

   Decide what additions you like and what you don't like. Keep what you like and place a check next to the dance ideas you are adding to your movement phrase or dance section.

2. If the movement problem has not already asked you to do this, you and your group add choreographic elements to manipulate (play with) the movement. Using the movement phrases, try the following:
   ___ Perform the movement phrase in unison (doing the same movement at the same time).
   ___ Choose your favorite movement and repeat it at various times during the phrase.
   ___ Do some of the movement at different levels (low, middle, high).
   ___ Change the tempo (speed) of some of the movements.
   ___ Do the movement so that it travels in a floor pattern.

   Decide what additions you like and what you don't like. Keep what you like and place a check next to the dance ideas you are adding to your movement phrase or dance section.

Using Choreographic Processes

Take parts of your movement phrase and try the following to make another dance section:

___ Choose movements that look the opposite of each other, and have two people or two smaller groups dance them at the same time (contrast).

(continued)

Form 5.4 Student Worksheet—Refinement Task: Playing With Your Movement Phrase or Dance Section from *Dance About Anything* by M. Sprague, H. Scheff, and S. McGreevy-Nichols, 2006, Champaign, IL: Human Kinetics.

As stated, part of the refinement task is evaluating the dance and making the needed revisions. Form 5.1, Evaluating What Works and What Does Not Work, will guide this evaluation process. Form 5.2, Self-Evaluation of Work, leads the older students through more complex thinking. If you wish to grade the writing on any of these worksheets, form 5.6, Writing Rubrics for Worksheets, is included on the CD-ROM. In addition, form 5.6 should be used by the students as they compose and revise their answers.

Form 5.5   Student Worksheet—Refinement Task: Putting It All Together

Name _____ Class _____ Date _____

Instructions

Now that your group and the other groups have solved the movement problems and made additions to your movement phrases or dance sections, you should have enough movement material to make (choreograph) a dance. Use form 4.2, Choreographic Structures Resource Sheet, to help you put your dance together.

1. If the movement problem has not already asked you to do this, you and your group may want to add a choreographic structure to your movement phrase or dance section.

   Write the structures you and your group tried:

   Write the structures you and your group decided to use (if any) in your movement phrase or dance section:

2. It is time to put all the dance sections together. Look at all the different groups' dance sections. Discuss and decide on an order for the dance sections. (You may want your teacher to help you with this decision.) Note: More than one dance section could be performed at one time. Write the order of the groups' dance sections here:

3. Try some of the choreographic structures to help you and your classmates organize the dance sections. Write the structures that you have decided to use in this dance.

4. Other ideas for designing your dance:
   - As you design your dance, keep in mind where your audience is sitting.
   - Explore different accompaniment for your dance, such as no sound, a narrative reading, or music.
   - Videotape your dance in its rough draft. Self-evaluate the dance and revise it as necessary.

Form 5.5 Student Worksheet—Refinement Task: Putting It All Together from *Dance About Anything* by M. Sprague, H. Scheff, and S. McGreevy-Nichols, 2006, Champaign, IL: Human Kinetics.

Form 5.6   Teacher Form—Development and Refinement Tasks: Writing Rubrics for Worksheets

	Incomplete: 0-1	Just beginning: 2	Working toward: 3	Complete work: 4	Above standard: 5	Peer or teacher score	Score on revised document
Content Note: Content score is counted twice. For example, for complete work, 4 × 2 = 8 points.	The work is too incomplete to grade. Many missing or incomplete answers.	Missing 2 or more answers and/or answers are incomplete. Examples or details from class are missing. There is little explanation to support answers or ideas. Not enough connections to class learning.	One question is not answered, or some answers lack specific examples or details from class. Explanations are general and do not clearly support answer or idea. Connection to class learning is unfocused.	All questions are answered with at least one specific example and detail from class. An explanation supports the answer or idea. Answer is reflective and connects to class learning.	All questions are answered with several specific examples or details from class. Thorough explanation supports answer or idea. Very thoughtful, reflective, original, and insightful.		
Structure of sentence and/or paragraphs	Writing is incomplete; there is little organization or focus to ideas.	Writing is incomplete; lacks organization and/or focus; the meaning is unclear; run-on sentences.	Writing is incomplete or does not make sense; needs organization; run-on or unfocused sentences.	Writing is complete and organized; makes sense and communicates ideas.	Writing is complete, organized, and meaningful; has very clear focus. Sentences include simple and complex variety.		
Spelling, grammar, and punctuation	Mistakes overpower the writing.	Mistakes often interfere with understanding.	Enough mistakes to occasionally interfere with understanding.	Few mistakes. Mistakes do not interfere with understanding of writing.	No mistakes in these areas. Writing about total content.		
					Total points (out of 20)		

Form 5.6 Teacher Form—Development and Refinement Tasks: Writing Rubrics for Worksheets from *Dance About Anything* by M. Sprague, H. Scheff, and S. McGreevy-Nichols, 2006, Champaign, IL: Human Kinetics.

Chapter 6

Exhibition Task: Performing Completed Work and Accepting Final Critique

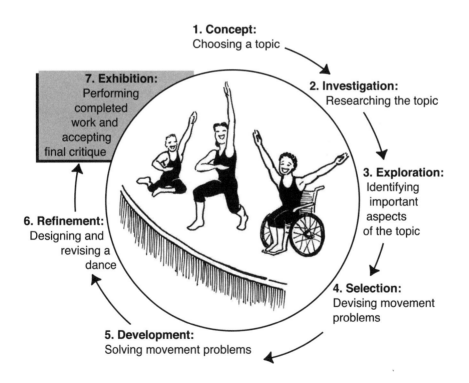

1. Concept:
Choosing a topic

2. Investigation:
Researching the topic

3. Exploration:
Identifying important aspects of the topic

4. Selection:
Devising movement problems

5. Development:
Solving movement problems

6. Refinement:
Designing and revising a dance

7. Exhibition:
Performing completed work and accepting final critique

The exhibition task in the choreographic process includes the final performance and the final critique of the dance. Dance is a performing art, so performing the created and crafted dance is necessary in order to complete the learning. At this level, all the cognitive processes (see table I.1 in the introduction, p. 2) include interaction with the feedback from others.

Performing the Completed Work

Once the final revisions are made and the dance is rehearsed, the exhibition or performance is held. Formal dance concerts can be a celebration of learning and serve as education and entertainment for the audience. Exhibitions can range from informal sharing sessions to large-scale productions. No matter the size of the production, performing the dances that you and your students have created completes the choreographic process.

Through performance, students gain physical and emotional power, self-esteem, and a sense of responsibility. After being performers themselves, they develop an appreciation for the arts. Performing involves higher-level thinking. Instantaneous problem

Dance concerts can be a celebration of student learning.

solving and decision making come into play because anything can happen during a performance. We have seen our performers deal effectively with forgotten steps, lost costumes and props, music and lighting mishaps, and even a fire drill. The value for the learning community is that students are often seen in a very different light. Resource teachers and policemen alike have asked us how we were able to get certain students to perform so beautifully. There is a value to your programming because the high level of learning is so clearly visible in the performance.

Creating, performing, and responding to dance are three basic cognitive processes found in many local, state, and national dance standards. As in all cognitive processes, they involve students in a series of actions that produce a specific result—in this case a dance. Performance, when approached as a process, encourages students to reflect on, revise, and perfect the performance of a given piece of choreography. This process encourages students to grow as creators, dancers, and performers. After the dance is created, consider the following performance process:

- Practice, practice, practice! Students should memorize and rehearse the choreography. If possible, videotape rehearsals so that students can use it to evaluate their progress. Give the students form 6.1, Helpful Rehearsal Strategies, to help them memorize and master their dances.

- Evaluate and refine. This is the time to have the students reflect on their performance of the piece and also their rehearsal habits. Students need to discuss any problems with the performance and suggest solutions to the problems.

Form 6.1   Student Handout—Exhibition Task: Helpful Rehearsal Strategies

The following are some general rehearsal strategies for all dances:

- Write down the dance and then use these notes to practice your dance correctly.
- Practice your steps with someone else.
- Have someone watch you and give you a critique (corrections).
- Work on the parts that you have the most trouble with.
- Create a rhythmic chant pattern to help you remember a difficult part. (For example, "When I do the box step, my hands go back.")
- Try to perform the dance without anyone's help.
- Use sweat equity—in other words, work hard.
- Memorize the words, music, counts, and visual cues as necessary to the performance of the dance.

The following are some rehearsal strategies for ensemble dances:

- Counts and movements need to be unified and exact.
- During unison sections, both impulses (initiation of movement) and breath rhythms (breathing that causes movement to be done in a certain way) among the dancers need to be synchronized.
- Focus and facial expressions are the same.
- Angles of facings are set.
- Leg and arm movements, even the height of the legs, are coordinated among all the dancers.

Form 6.1 Student Handout—Exhibition Task: Helpful Rehearsal Strategies from *Dance About Anything* by M. Sprague, H. Scheff, and S. McGreevy-Nichols, 2006, Champaign, IL: Human Kinetics. Adapted, by permission, from H. Scheff, M. Sprague, and S. McGreevy-Nichols, 2005, *Experiencing Dance: From Student to Dance Artist* (Champaign, IL: Human Kinetics), 157-158.

Adapted, by permission, from H. Scheff, M. Sprague, and S. McGreevy-Nichols, 2005, *Experiencing dance: From student to dance artist* (Champaign, IL: Human Kinetics), 157-158.

- Final performance—it's showtime! Give the students form 6.2, Helpful Performance Strategies, to help them have a successful performance. Videotape the performance. If you do not have the equipment, borrow it or seek help from parents or colleagues and have them videotape the performance for you.

Form 6.2   Student Handout—Exhibition Task: Helpful Performance Strategies

The following are some performance strategies:

- Always warm up.
- Review problem spots in your dances.
- Concentrate. Do your work.
- Find some quiet time to help you remain calm and focused.
- Be quiet in and around the performing area.
- Before your entrances, get into character (the correct quality of movement).
- If you make a mistake, continue on as if nothing has happened.
- When exiting, continue performing until you are well past the wings and exit area.

Form 6.2 Student Handout—Exhibition Task: Helpful Performance Strategies from *Dance About Anything* by M. Sprague, H. Scheff, and S. McGreevy-Nichols, 2006, Champaign, IL: Human Kinetics. Adapted, by permission, from H. Scheff, M. Sprague, and S. McGreevy-Nichols, 2005, *Experiencing Dance: From Student to Dance Artist* (Champaign, IL: Human Kinetics), 158.

Adapted, by permission, from H. Scheff, M. Sprague, and S. McGreevy-Nichols, 2005, *Experiencing dance: From student to dance artist* (Champaign, IL: Human Kinetics), 158.

Accepting and Using the Final Critique

Choreographers use **critiques** (observations, corrections, and comments) on their "finished" dances in one of three ways: They can use the critique to improve the dance for its next performance, they can use the critique to improve their work on the next dance, or they can choose to ignore the criticism and leave the dance in its original form. After the performance of your dance, you and your students have the same options.

- Reflection after the performance is as important as any of the other tasks in the choreographic process. Often students have the opportunity to perform the piece more than once. The performers must be given time to reflect on their work. Improvements to the dance can be noted and revisions can be made before the dance is performed again. Even if there are no plans for a repeat performance, students can benefit from reflecting on how they can improve their overall choreographic and performance ability. (See form 6.3, Student Performance Assessment Form.)

- Performances can be assessed through the use of self-evaluation and peer evaluation as well as evaluation by audience members and your teaching team. All of these resources will give students a complete picture of their work. Videotaping the dances is an essential tool for evaluation, documentation, and advocacy. (See form 6.4, Video or Performance Critique.) It is worth your time to raise funds or invest part of your school budget to obtain the necessary equipment for videotaping.

- For self-evaluation and peer evaluation, students have to be taught to respond to and deliver feedback appropriately. You have to teach them how to look objectively at their own work and others' work. If you are using a videotape of their performance for reflection purposes, it is helpful if you show the video to them more than once. The

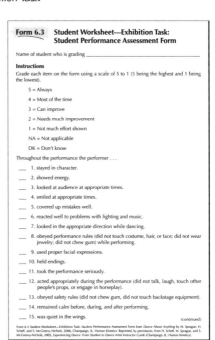

Form 6.3 Student Worksheet—Exhibition Task: Student Performance Assessment Form

Name of student who is grading _____

Instructions

Grade each item on the form using a scale of 5 to 1 (5 being the highest and 1 being the lowest).

 5 = Always

 4 = Most of the time

 3 = Can improve

 2 = Needs much improvement

 1 = Not much effort shown

 NA = Not applicable

 DK = Don't know

Throughout the performance the performer . . .

___ 1. stayed in character.

___ 2. showed energy.

___ 3. looked at audience at appropriate times.

___ 4. smiled at appropriate times.

___ 5. covered up mistakes well.

___ 6. reacted well to problems with lighting and music.

___ 7. looked in the appropriate direction while dancing.

___ 8. obeyed performance rules (did not touch costume, hair, or face; did not wear jewelry; did not chew gum) while performing.

___ 9. used proper facial expressions.

___ 10. held endings.

___ 11. took the performance seriously.

___ 12. acted appropriately during the performance (did not talk, laugh, touch other people's props, or engage in horseplay).

___ 13. obeyed safety rules (did not chew gum, did not touch backstage equipment).

___ 14. remained calm before, during, and after performing.

___ 15. was quiet in the wings. *(continued)*

Form 6.3 Student Worksheet—Exhibition Task: Student Performance Assessment Form from *Dance About Anything* by M. Sprague, H. Scheff, and S. McGreevy-Nichols, 2006, Champaign, IL: Human Kinetics. Reprinted, by permission, from H. Scheff, M. Sprague, and S. McGreevy-Nichols, 2005, *Experiencing Dance: From Student to Dance Artist Instructor Guide* (Champaign, IL: Human Kinetics).

Reprinted, by permission, from H. Scheff, M. Sprague, and S. McGreevy-Nichols, 2005, *Experiencing dance: From student to dance artist instructor guide* (Champaign, IL: Human Kinetics).

Form 6.4 Student Worksheet—Exhibition Task: Video or Performance Critique

Name _____ Class _____ Date _____

Instructions

Either answer these questions in writing or use them for a discussion about the dance.

 1. What was the name of the dance that you watched?

 2. Who was the choreographer?

 3. What was the style of dance being performed (modern, jazz, tap, ballet, world dance, folk, other)?

 4. What did you like most about the dance and why?

 5. What did you like least about the dance and why?

 6. Describe what the dancers did well.

 7. Describe where in the dance that the dancers need more rehearsal.

(continued)

Form 6.4 Student Worksheet—Exhibition Task: Video or Performance Critique from *Dance About Anything* by M. Sprague, H. Scheff, and S. McGreevy-Nichols, 2006, Champaign, IL: Human Kinetics.

first viewing will help students get over the shock of seeing themselves on a television screen. The students will be able to be more objective during the second showing of the dance. When evaluating choreography, students have to be reminded to look at the structure of the dance. When they evaluate performances, give students a list of criteria to help them stay objective (see form 6.5, Evaluation of Dance Performance Quality Resource Sheet). Remind them to deliver their critique in positive and helpful language. Require them to support their comments and opinions with further explanations and details from the dance. Students on the receiving end of a critique can learn from their successes and mistakes.

- You can pass out evaluations to the audience to get them to evaluate the dances (see form 6.6, Audience Evaluation of Performance) and give them instructions to leave the completed evaluations with the ushers. Explain the importance of the evaluations to the students. We used to read

Form 6.5 Student Handout—Exhibition Task: Evaluation of Dance Performance Quality Resource Sheet

When evaluating your own or someone else's performance, you should look for the following:

- Appropriate amount of energy in all movements
- Clarity of movements (are the movements clearly performed, not wishy-washy?)
- Spacing: personal spacing and group spacing (are the dancers where they should be?)
- Confidence and preparedness (did the dancer seem to know what to do and when, or did the dancer follow other dancers?)
- Concentration: no talking, giggling, making faces, fussing with costumes; the dancer is focusing on the dance
- Memorization of movements, entrances, and exits
- Attention to music or sound score (does it seem that the dancer is on the correct count or cue?)
- Continuation of the movement all the way off the stage (were the exits cleanly done?)
- Focus was not on the floor unless it seems as if the movement requires the dancer to look down
- Silence in the wing space (there is no distracting noise from backstage)
- Obvious commitment to performing the dance well (the dancer is not just going through the motions)

Form 6.5 Student Handout—Exhibition Task: Evaluation of Dance Performance Quality Resource Sheet from *Dance About Anything* by M. Sprague, H. Scheff, and S. McGreevy-Nichols, 2006, Champaign, IL: Human Kinetics.

Form 6.6 Audience Worksheet—Exhibition Task: Audience Evaluation of Performance

Name of show _____ Date _____

Audience member's name (optional but helpful) _____

Use the following scale to evaluate the students:

(+): The students demonstrated the following criteria during the entire performance.

(✓): The students demonstrated the following criteria during most of the performance.

(–): The students did not demonstrate the following criteria enough to make the performance successful.

1. _____ Knowledge of the dances

The students performed with clarity. Movements were clearly memorized. Students knew what they were doing and where and when to come on and off the stage. Students moved together (when they apparently were supposed to be in unison, they were moving at the same time or on the beat of music).

Your comments:

2. _____ Quality of performance

Students performed in character. They focused on the audience. They smiled when appropriate and showed other facial emotions when necessary. They were able to keep dancing even if something unplanned happened on stage. They made you want to watch them.

Your comments:

3. _____ Professional and appropriate behavior

Students were quiet during dances and during exits and entrances. They took their job seriously. They weren't just going through the motions. They demonstrated respect for each other and for the audience.

Your comments:

Form 6.6 Audience Worksheet—Exhibition Task: Audience Evaluation of Performance from *Dance About Anything* by M. Sprague, H. Scheff, and S. McGreevy-Nichols, 2006, Champaign, IL: Human Kinetics. Adapted from H. Scheff, M. Sprague, and S. McGreevy-Nichols, 2005, *Experiencing Dance: From Student to Dance Artist Instructor Guide* (Champaign, IL: Human Kinetics), handout for lesson 11.3—Take a Bow: Exhibiting Strength, Flexibility, and Endurance in Performance.

Adapted from H. Scheff, M. Sprague, and S. McGreevy-Nichols, 2005, *Experiencing dance: From student to dance artist instructor guide* (Champaign, IL: Human Kinetics), handout for lesson 11.3—Take a Bow: Exhibiting Strength, Flexibility, and Endurance in Performance.

the audience evaluations to our students before the next show. (We usually had multiple performances of the same shows.) The students were held accountable for making the corrections to their performances.

Feedback from the different sources can also be used as a final assessment for both your teaching and your students' work. We have used audience evaluations, teacher evaluations, self-evaluations, and peer evaluations to grade students on their choreographic and performing skills. Each time we have taught choreography or implemented an integrated project, we have learned from all of these types of evaluations and have improved our content and instruction.

Using the Exhibition Task Worksheets and Handouts

The exhibition task worksheets and handouts are meant to help you and your students have successful performances. Form 6.1, Helpful Rehearsal Strategies, gives suggestions for rehearsing dances in preparation for a performance, while form 6.2, Helpful Performance Strategies, gives helpful suggestions for performing. If necessary, you can use the information on these handouts to teach these strategies to the younger students. Form 6.3, Student Performance Assessment Form, is useful for evaluating a student's performance skills and behavior during the performance. Finally, form 6.4, Video or Performance Critique, is to be used as written work or as a base for the discussion about a dance and its performance.

Adapted from H. Scheff, M. Sprague, and S. McGreevy-Nichols, 2005, *Experiencing dance: From student to dance artist instructor guide* (Champaign, IL: Human Kinetics), handout for lesson 11.3—Take a Bow: Class or Rehearsal Evaluation.

Form 6.7   Student Worksheet—Exhibition Task: Evaluation of Class or Rehearsal

Name _____ Class _____ Date _____

[ ] Teacher [ ] Self [ ] Peer: Name of peer being evaluated _____

Use the following scales to evaluate the student:

(+): This student always displayed good and acceptable work in the criteria listed.

(✓): This student always displayed good and acceptable work the majority of the time for most of the criteria listed.

(–): This student did not meet the expectations for the activity, behavior, or criteria listed.

1. ___ This person demonstrated manners in class and rehearsal in the following ways:
   • Acted maturely (didn't disturb others, had self-control, didn't waste time).
   • Gave respect to the teacher and to other students.
   • Stayed on task (kept on working independently, was patient when it wasn't his or her turn, practiced on own while teacher was with someone else).
   • Listened to and watched the teacher or peer leader carefully and asked questions when confused.

2. ___ This person participated in class or rehearsal to the best of his or her abilities:
   • Clearly was memorizing movement, counts, spacing, entrances, exits, and so on.
   • Fixed mistakes when corrected by peers or by the teacher.
   • Kept trying and didn't give up when the movement seemed difficult.

3. ___ This person showed responsibility in attendance of class or rehearsals:
   • Learned any dance steps missed during an absence.
   • Demonstrated, through dancing, that he or she practiced before the class or rehearsal.
   • Participated fully in the warm-up technique and conditioning parts of the class.

4. ___ This person danced with the necessary energy and clarity:
   • Danced full out whenever required by the teacher; rehearsed as if it were a performance.
   • Used appropriate acting and facial expressions when required.
   • Willing to work hard, fix and repeat dance phrases until they were corrected, and sweat!

5. ___ This person demonstrated good teamwork:
   • Worked easily with others and cooperated on group and team decisions.
   • Helped other dancers whenever needed.
   • Shared ideas with team or group and participated in making up movement phrases when necessary.
   • Was well focused and open to suggestions and ideas.

Form 6.7 Student Worksheet—Exhibition Task: Evaluation of Class or Rehearsal from *Dance About Anything* by M. Sprague, H. Scheff, and S. McGreevy-Nichols, 2006, Champaign, IL: Human Kinetics. Adapted from H. Scheff, M. Sprague, and S. McGreevy-Nichols, 2005, *Experiencing Dance: From Student to Dance Artist Instructor Guide* (Champaign, IL: Human Kinetics), handout for lesson 11.3—Take a Bow: Class or Rehearsal Evaluation.

The exhibition task worksheets and handouts will also help you and your students get and use feedback on the dance and performance. Form 6.5, Evaluation of Dance Performance Quality Resource Sheet, will help students know what to look for when evaluating either their own or others' performances. To get feedback from the audience, use form 6.6, Audience Evaluation of Performance. You and your students will glean helpful information about the performance of your dances. Form 6.7, Evaluation of Class or Rehearsal, is a worksheet for self-evaluation and peer evaluation as well as evaluation by the teacher. This evaluation will determine the quality of the students' work in dance classes or rehearsals.

Using the Dance Designing Activity Cards

Dance Designing Activity Cards (forms 6.8-6.15, included on the CD-ROM) are vehicles for creating dances. The instructions take the students through the seven tasks of the choreographic process. At the end of the activity, your students will have a complete dance.

The topic gives the concept or inspiration for the dance. Materials that are needed are listed. Before the activity, you, as teacher, may need to collect these resources for the students. Student work is the product that students must produce. Instructions are given to guide the students through the choreographic process. Dance design suggestions are smaller selections or aspects of the larger topic about which students can dance. Standards list the areas in which students can meet expectations. Please refer to the standards approved by your district. The rubric tells you and the students what level of work is expected.

Included on the CD-ROM is a detailed Dance Designing Activity Card (form 6.16) illustrating what to include in each section. Also included on the CD-ROM is a blank Dance Designing Activity Card (form 6.17). Using this format, you can create your own dance designing activities.

You, as a teacher, may be called on to do direct teaching and to step back to facilitate and coach your students through their choreographic experience. For more information on teaching, facilitating, and coaching, see chapter 9. By using the Flight Dance Designing Activities, you and your students will produce a fine dance and learn much about creativity and the choreographic process. Included at the end of this chapter are the three grade levels' (K to 4, 5 to 8, 9 to 12) Flight Dance Designing Activities in table format (tables 6.1-6.3). The documents are aligned with the seven tasks of the choreographic process.

Table 6.1   Flight Dance Designing Activity As It Relates to Tasks of Choreographic Process (Grades K to 4)

Task	Dance designing activity
Concept task	Dance Designing Activity (Grades K to 4) Topic: Flight Student work: Create a dance or dance section using the following quote.
Investigation task	Instructions: 1. Read the following information about the way birds fly. Four forces are at work when an object, such as a bird or plane, is in flight: **gravity, lift, drag,** and **thrust.** Birds use these forces and other movements to take off, land, glide, soar, and travel short and long distances. All objects are pulled down to earth by **gravity.** Birds adjust to the effects of gravity with the special design of their bodies. Birds have hollow bones and lightweight feathers so that they are light enough to fly. All birds have wings. Wings allow birds to fly. The feathers on the wings create a shape called an *airfoil.* As a bird moves through the air, its wing structure causes the air to flow faster above the wing, resulting in lower air pressure, while the air under the wing flows more slowly, resulting in higher air pressure. This difference in airflow gives the bird **lift.** Birds can also get lift by flying into the wind. The wind, however, slows their forward movement, so birds adjust by turning slightly from time to time.

(continued)

Table 6.1 *(continued)*

Task	Dance designing activity
	An object experiences resistance as it flies. This is the same sensation that you feel against your arm when you stick it out the window as you ride in a car. This force is called **drag.** Birds account for drag by adjusting the shape and movement of their wings. When a large surface area of the wing is exposed to oncoming wind, it slows the bird down; when less surface is exposed, the bird moves faster.
	When birds take off, they use several strategies to lift them into the air. Birds change the angle of their wings, spread their feathers to create slots, use the wind, and increase speed by flapping. When birds want to land, they adjust their wings to create more drag. The tail is spread open and lowered to act as a brake.
	Soaring and flapping help to keep birds in the air. Birds use different kinds of air conditions to help them soar. Thermal air currents (warm air that rises above cold air in various heating conditions), updrafts (air that rises as it rushes over an obstruction like a mountain or a high building), and wind moving toward the bird all provide ways for birds to glide through the air without using a lot of energy. When soaring, birds usually fly in circles, spiraling up in the rising air.
	Birds can also move forward by flapping their wings. This forward motion is called **thrust.** Birds generate thrust with every flap of their wings. As birds flap their wings, the wing tips move forward and downward and then loop around, moving upward and backward. This motion, combined with wing design, adjusts the pressure around the wing and moves the bird forward.
	Birds can turn in many ways. Some use their tails as rudders, opening and closing their tail feathers while moving the tail up and down. Others bank as they turn, tilting one wing higher than the other. Some birds turn by beating one wing faster than the other.
	Talk with your teacher if you need help understanding any of these ideas.
	Sources:
	http://wings.avkids.com/Book/Animals/intermediate/birds-01.html
	www.provet.co.uk/kids/kids%20questions/kqbirdflight.htm
	www.furball.warbirdsiii.com/krod/basic-physics.html
	www.learner.org/jnorth/tm/crane/flightlesson.html

Exploration task	2. Complete form 3.4, Idea and Word Sort for Categories.
	3. Make a movement phrase based on some of the words in one of your categories.
	4. Repeat step 3 until you have created a movement phrase for each of your categories.
	5. Decide which movement phrases are either your best or your favorites.
Selection task	6. Using form 4.1, Dance Ideas List, and thinking about your categories and movement phrases, choose the best movement skills and locomotor, nonlocomotor, and movement qualities.
Development task	7. Add these movements to your movement phrases.
	8. Using form 5.4, Playing With Your Movement Phrase or Dance Section, add more movement to your dance.
Refinement task	9. Choose an order for your movement phrases. Create a dance that shows how and why birds move in special ways. Do additional research as needed. The dance should represent a variety of bird movements.
	10. Get feedback from your teacher and classmates and revise your dance.
	11. You may add music or a sound score that fits your movement and topic.
	12. Practice your dance or section of the dance.
Exhibition task	13. Perform your dance.
	14. Ask your audience what they liked about your dance and what you could improve in your dance.
	15. Rubric:
	(+): Students have contributed 5 or 6 movement phrases to the dance or section of the dance. The dance or dance section is well developed, organized, and complete.
	(✓): Students have contributed 3 or 4 movement phrases to the dance or section of the dance. The dance or dance section is developed and has a sense of being complete.
	(–): Students have contributed only 1 or 2 movement phrases to the dance or section of the dance and/or the dance or dance sections are unclear or underdeveloped and need much revision.

(continued)

Table 6.1 *(continued)*

Task	Dance designing activity
	At the end of this activity, you will have a complete dance or section of a dance. A dance or dance section has a beginning (shape, entrance, or movement), a middle (development or exploration of idea), and an end (shape, exit, or movement).

Standards to be met by student work: teamwork; dance (use of choreographic elements, benchmarks for structures and processes); English language arts; reading comprehension; and science.

Table 6.2 Flight Dance Designing Activity As It Relates to Tasks of Choreographic Process (Grades 5 to 8)

Task	Dance designing activity
Concept task	Dance Designing Activity (Grades 5 to 8) Topic: Flight Student work: Create a dance based on the following image and your research. Instructions: 1. Look at the image. Use it as your topic or inspiration for your dance.
Investigation task	2. Do research on the identified flight concepts and find out how they apply to the flight of birds and to the flight of airplanes.
Exploration task	3. Compare and contrast the flight abilities of birds and airplanes. To do this, use a two-column compare-and-contrast list or a Venn diagram.
Selection task	4. From form 4.1, Dance Ideas List, choose dance ideas that are best for the different sections of the dance. In other words, choose the dance ideas that best show bird flight and the dance ideas that best show airplane flight. If you want to show the aspects of flight that birds and airplanes share (from the center of the Venn diagram), choose still other dance ideas from the list.
Development task	5. Develop your dance sections by adding the dance ideas that you chose for the different sections of the dance. Carry out the plan that you made in instruction 4.

Refinement task	6. Use the AB choreographic structure if you want to show a simple comparison and contrast of the flight of birds and airplanes. Use the rondo (ABACA) choreographic structure if you want to stress the shared aspects of flight for both birds and airplanes (as A), and use sections B and C for the flight of birds and airplanes, respectively. See form 4.2, Choreographic Structures Resource Sheet, for further information on these two choreographic structures. 7. Get feedback from your teacher and classmates and revise your dance. 8. If you wish, you may add music or a sound score that fits your movement and topic. 9. Practice your dance or dance section.
Exhibition task	10. Perform your dance. 11. Ask your audience what they liked about your dance and what you could improve in your dance. Have your peers watch your dance and fill out form 6.4, Video or Performance Critique. 12. Rubric: (+): Students have contributed 5 or 6 movement phrases to the dance or section of the dance. The dance or dance section is well developed, organized, and complete. (✓): Students have contributed 3 or 4 movement phrases to the dance or section of the dance. The dance or dance section is developed and has a sense of being complete. (–): Students have contributed only 1 or 2 movement phrases to the dance or section of the dance and/or the dance or dance sections are unclear or underdeveloped and need much revision.
	At the end of this activity, you will have a complete dance or section of a dance. A dance or dance section has a beginning (shape, entrance, or movement), a middle (development or exploration of idea), and an end (shape, exit, or movement).

Standards to be met by student work: teamwork; dance (use of choreographic elements, benchmarks for structures and processes); English language arts; reading comprehension; and science.

Table 6.3   Flight Dance Designing Activity As It Relates to Tasks of Choreographic Process (Grades 9 to 12)

Task	Dance designing activity
Concept task	Dance Designing Activity (Grades 9 to 12) Topic: Flight Student work: Create a dance about Newton's first law as it pertains to flight. (Other dance designing suggestions: Research the rest of Newton's laws. Create a dance for each law that communicates its relationship with flight.)
Investigation task	Instructions: 1. Look at the illustration and read the text. **Newton's first law** applied to airplanes — Glenn Research Center Airspeed Thrust ← [airplane illustration] → Drag "Every object persists in its state of rest or uniform motion in a straight line unless it is compelled to change that state by forces impressed on it." *When flying at a constant altitude:* If thrust and drag are equal, aircraft holds constant airspeed. *If thrust is increased:* Aircraft accelerates – airspeed increases Drag depends on airspeed – drag increases *When drag is again equal to thrust:* Aircraft no longer accelerates but holds a new, higher, constant airspeed. Reprinted from www.grc.nasa.gov/WWW/K-12/airplane/newton1.htm.
Exploration task	2. Complete form 3.2, Images, Events, Messages, and Words Taken From Research for Movement Prompts. If necessary, conduct more research to give you a better understanding or more ideas.
Selection task	3. Working in a small group, use form 3.6, Using Text to Make Movement; form 4.1, Dance Ideas List; and form 4.5, Designing Movement Problems, to make a written movement problem for your topic.

Development task	4. Trade movement problems with another group. Solve their movement problem and have them solve yours. You will then have two movement phrases or dance sections.
Refinement task	5. Use form 5.5, Putting It All Together, to develop and organize the dance sections to make a complete dance. 6. Evaluate and make revisions to your dance. You can use form 5.1, Evaluating What Works and What Does Not Work. 7. If you wish, you may add music or a sound score that fits your movement and topic. 8. Practice your dance.
Exhibition task	9. Perform your dance. 10. Ask your audience what they liked about your dance and what you could improve in your dance. Have your peers watch your dance and fill out form 6.6, Audience Evaluation of Performance. 11. Rubric: (+): Students have contributed 5 or 6 movement phrases to the dance or section of the dance. The dance or dance section is well developed, organized, and complete. (✓): Students have contributed 3 or 4 movement phrases to the dance or section of the dance. The dance or dance section is developed and has a sense of being complete. (–): Students have contributed only 1 or 2 movement phrases to the dance or section of the dance and/or the dance or dance sections are unclear or underdeveloped and need much revision.
	At the end of this activity, you will have a complete dance or section of a dance. A dance or dance section has a beginning (shape, entrance, or movement), a middle (development or exploration of idea), and an end (shape, exit, or movement).

Standards to be met by student work: teamwork; dance (use of choreographic elements, benchmarks for structures and processes); English language arts; reading comprehension; and science.

Summary of Part II

In part II, we take you through the last four tasks of the choreographic process: selection task, development task, refinement task, and exhibition task. After students have chosen the important aspects of a topic, they can create a full dance based on these aspects. We equip you to lead your students through devising movement problems, solving them (resulting in movement phrases or dance sections), designing and revising a dance, performing the completed dance, and accepting the final critique of the dance. You and your students are no longer novices. As you repeat these seven tasks several times, in each new dance project you and your students will become more and more adept at the choreographic process.

Part III

Integrated Projects
From Thematic
Planning to Exhibition

In chapter 7, we define, in depth, what constitutes an integrated project. You are also informed about creating and writing an integrated project. Chapter 8 contains practical information to help get your project going and keep it on target, including where and how to seek help with team building, resources, and funding. Chapter 9 explains how effective teaching, facilitating, and coaching can engage and keep students' interest. Chapter 10 relates the learning in integrated projects with life and work skills. The text and worksheets focus on the larger sphere of learning that integrated projects should address.

At the end of chapter 7 (pp. 97-100) you will find a complete copy of the Flight Integrated Project. It appears as a table highlighting the seven tasks of the cognitive processes.

Chapter 7

Defining and Creating Integrated Projects: The Process Is the Process

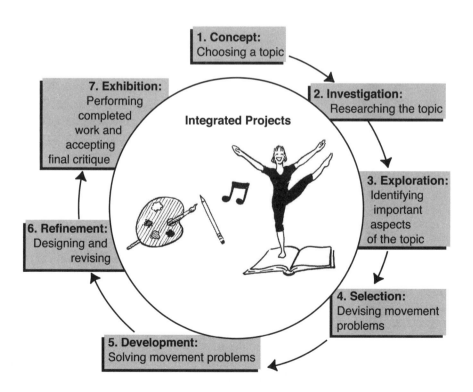

1. **Concept:** Choosing a topic

2. **Investigation:** Researching the topic

3. **Exploration:** Identifying important aspects of the topic

4. **Selection:** Devising movement problems

5. **Development:** Solving movement problems

6. **Refinement:** Designing and revising

7. **Exhibition:** Performing completed work and accepting final critique

Integrated Projects

In this chapter we take an in-depth look at what constitutes an integrated project. We then take you through the process of creating an integrated project—using the same steps and thinking process that you explored in parts I and II—and writing the document that will act as a script during its implementation with your students. Note that chapters 7 and 8 should be read in tandem. Chapter 7 deals with creating and writing an integrated project for your students, and chapter 8 deals with the practical aspects in creating and implementing the projects.

Integrated Projects: Defined

Integrate means to bring together or incorporate (parts) into a whole. Relating this to **integrated projects** means that various subject areas are brought together and the learning is approached as a whole. For example, a study can be made of the community in which the school is located. Social studies, geography, visual arts, music, folk art, English language arts, economics, teamwork, applied learning, home and consumer science, and of course dance would be part of the integrated project. The student learning is not segmented by subject area; rather, it flows freely from subject area to subject area as the work requires.

In education, dance can be used in a variety of ways:

- Dance can be taught as a specific arts discipline.
- Dance can help you teach other subject areas.
- Dance can be taught through integrated projects.

In an integrated project, dance can be the major focus, driving the work in all subject areas. Our integrated project of Anna and the King (see chapter 13) demonstrates how dance can drive different parts of an integrated project. Dance can also play a smaller role in an integrated project. In Community Quilt (see chapter 12), dance is included only in the exhibition segment of the integrated project.

Integrated projects usually have an overarching theme that links various subjects. David Perkins (1989, p. 75) states, "First, an integrative theme engages students in a thoughtful confrontation with the subject matters. . . . Moreover, attention to the integrative theme fosters a level of abstraction in students' thinking that they are otherwise not likely to reach."

The following becomes most important in integrated projects:

- Many skills and concepts are learned, which can then be applied to any subject. With so much to be learned, this is an efficient approach.
- The learning is connected across subjects and to students' lives. Learning is enriched, personalized, and not fragmented.
- Student interest is engaged. Since the students have input into the project, it is fun and meaningful for them.

Creating integrated projects may seem work intensive; however, the learning that takes place is powerful. It is not surprising that integrated projects (units) have become a staple of the elementary curriculum and are prominent in the middle and high school reform initiatives. With all the content that teachers are required to cover, integrated teaching simply makes sense and is a more natural way for students to learn.

Using the Creative Process to Create Integrated Projects

We have explained how to use the creative process to make dances. Teachers can use the components of this process (the concept task, investigation task, exploration task, selection task, development task, refinement task, and exhibition task) to create integrated projects. After all, it takes a great deal of creativity to combine an assortment of subject content and curricular requirements into a motivating and fun project. The following sections explain how to accomplish this feat.

Concept Task: Choosing a Topic and Outlining a Plan

The topic that you choose depends on a number of factors, such as specific standards or other educational outcomes that need to be met, curricular content you want to cover, specific student needs that have to be met, and students' interests as well as your own interests. For example, in the integrated project Community Quilt that we facilitated at Roger Williams Middle School (see chapter 12), the students expressed an interest in finding out more about the people in their immediate community. Despite the cultural diversity that exists in our neighborhood, each ethnic group lives fairly insular lives. The students wanted to learn about and understand each other's traditions. This topic can work for you even if your school is not apparently multicultural. Every student's family has a cultural background that can be investigated and explored. This topic satisfies students' interest. It easily lends itself to meeting a variety of standards, such as English language arts, social studies, applied learning, visual arts, and dance. The ability to meet these standards depends on how the student work is designed (which we will consider in the selection task and development task). Obviously this topic can satisfy many curricular aspects and themes such as knowing your community, the aspects of creating and performing in both dance and the visual arts, and reading and writing. Integrated projects help make connections between subjects. Do several of your students have low test scores in reading comprehension? This student need can be addressed in the project through multiple student tasks.

Use the concept task to map out the integrated project by setting up the basic outline for the rest of your work. We incorporate the basics of backward planning, a practice used by many school districts. Backward planning starts with selecting standards as the desired outcome, identifying acceptable evidence of having met the standards (the students' work), and planning the teaching required to support the work. This approach is embedded within the project design process.

The following sidebar shows a brief outline for the Flight Integrated Project. See table 7.1 for a full description of the Flight Integrated Project. As you can see, the standards to be met in this project are primarily in the areas of dance, English language arts, and science. Specific standards and benchmarks within these content areas will need to be identified, which will depend on particular state and local standards being addressed and the specific grade. In the outline, you also will see the large piece of student work to be produced.

Project Title: Come Fly With Me

I. Standards to be met: dance, physical science, and English language arts (specific to states and grades).

II. Major piece of student work: Students create a grade-appropriate lecture/demonstration that explains, with the help of dance, one of the following concepts: the power of air, overcoming gravity, laws of motion, forces of flight (lift, propulsion, weight, and drag), how birds fly, and wing function and structure. See grade-specific examples: how birds fly (grades K to 4), forces of flight (grades 5 to 8), and Newton's law of motion (grades 9 to 12).

Investigation Task: Researching the Topic

Once you have decided on a topic and developed an outline of a plan, it is time to research the chosen topic. As explained in chapter 2, there are several ways to investigate a topic. It will be helpful to review this information. You will need to do some initial research and identify some specific resources for students to use. The more facts that you have on the topic, the richer the experience will be. Thorough research allows you to find more options.

Next, you will need to research student resources. These are the materials that the students will use during the investigation task or research phase of the project. You will need to explore printed resources at your school and local libraries. You will also need to explore available Web sites on your chosen topic and research community resources, such as museums and local experts. Do you need to locate a book on the topic that all students can read? A visit to the local bookstore is a great place to start. At this point, you may want to devise a preproject questionnaire, which will be used to determine students' prior knowledge concerning the topic. Later this same questionnaire can be used as a posttest. Want more ideas? Use form 2.2, List of Research Resources, from chapter 2.

When researching for the flight project, you might collect a variety of books, videos, and DVDs on these specific topics: how birds fly (grades K to 4), the forces of flight (grades 5 to 8), and Newton's law of motion (grades 9 to 12). You can place these materials in a container so that they can be readily available for students' use throughout the implementation of the project. You should research and bookmark Web sites that will be useful to students' research. Local bird and aviation experts and sites for possible field trips are other useful resources.

Exploration Task: Narrowing the Focus

It is time to look at the collected information that you have gathered on your topic and narrow it to a more specific focus. This process naturally leads to the development of a focusing or guiding question. The purpose of a guiding question is to "hook" students' interest and to provide a pathway to lead students into the topic. The major piece of work in the project should contain the answer to the focusing or guiding question. Students' input is important at this time, particularly because contributing their ideas will keep them motivated. Remember that the question should be open-ended enough to allow for a variety of answers. Please note that if the focusing or guiding question is not working, don't be afraid to change it.

In the Flight Integrated Project the focusing or guiding question is "How can we show the concept of flight through an integrated dance project?" This question can be fine-tuned as work on the project progresses.

Selection Task: Designing Rigorous Student Work

The selection task concentrates on fleshing out the major piece of student work needed for the project. Specifically, this is a comprehensive and rigorous piece of work that satisfies multiple standards and student outcomes. Examples of this type of work are a dance or theater production, an art exhibit, a report, or a cultural event. This large piece of work usually is exhibited in some public forum.

This piece of work requires a rubric that will help the students succeed. Remember that your rubric is only as good as your criteria. The criteria for this piece of work must clearly define how you want the piece to look, address the standards to be met, spell out curricular requirements, and include any other class requirements such as a due date or suggested format. Review the planning that you did for the concept task so that you can remember the direction of the student work and proceed accordingly. Again, students can be instrumental in developing these criteria, and this is yet another way to get their buy-in. If you need more help developing criteria and rubrics, refer to *Building More Dances* (McGreevy-Nichols, Scheff, & Sprague, 2001), which devotes an entire chapter to this subject. Also refer to the section titled Assessment in the introduction to this book (pp. 10-12).

In the Flight Integrated Project, the major piece of student work is a lecture/demonstration (see the following sidebar).

Student Work 5: Major Piece of Student Work

Using both the dance sections and the oral report sections, students put their lecture/demonstrations together.

Assessment: Lecture/demonstrations are videotaped for self-evaluations and peer evaluations. Both the teacher and students create the rubric for the lecture/demonstrations; it will be based on physical science, English language arts, and dance standards.

Teaching required: Teacher facilitates the creation of the rubric. Teacher makes suggestions, as needed, for the best organization for the delivery of the lecture/demonstrations.

Development Tasks: Breaking Down the Learning

Now that you have decided on the major piece of student work, it is time to figure out what smaller pieces of student work will be needed. This work must scaffold, or build on, each element and be sequentially relevant to the larger piece of work. The smaller pieces should be critical components of the major piece of work. For example, in the Flight Integrated Project, smaller tasks include making movement sections and oral report sections. These will be linked together to explain the flight concepts that will be communicated in the lecture/demonstration.

Again, you will need to consider how you will assess each piece of student work. This does not always require a rubric, but students need to have their work acknowledged in some way even if it means just filing it in their portfolios. Portfolios are a great way to document all aspects of the student work and a way to organize all the elements. If you need more information about portfolios, see pages 36 and 37 of *Building More Dances* (McGreevy-Nichols, Scheff, & Sprague, 2001). In the following sidebar are examples of these smaller pieces of work.

Smaller Pieces of Work

Student Work 1

In small groups, students will research their grade-appropriate topic.

Assessment: Students will hand in note cards or form 2.3, Sources and Notes, for portfolio evidence.

Teaching required: Teacher will gather research materials or bookmark appropriate Web sites and instruct students in research strategies.

Student Work 2

Students will do the Flight Inspiration Activity in one class period.

- See Flight Inspiration Activity for grades K to 4 (table 3.2, p. 41).
- See Flight Inspiration Activity for grades 5 to 8 (table 3.3, p. 42).
- See Flight Inspiration Activity for grades 9 to 12 (table 3.4, p. 43).

Assessment: Students will produce movement phrases that demonstrate an understanding of the concept of flight.

Teaching required: Teacher facilitates the inspiration activity.

Student Work 3

Students do the Flight Dance Designing Activity in three or four class periods.

- See Flight Dance Designing Activity for grades K to 4 (table 6.1, pp. 75-78).
- See Flight Dance Designing Activity for grades 5 to 8 (table 6.2, pp. 78-79).
- See Flight Dance Designing Activity for grades 9 to 12 (table 6.3, pp. 80-81).

Assessment: Movement problems (in the dance designing activity) are solved according to the instructions to make a dance section or a complete dance on flight. Students should critique each other regarding how well the movement problems were solved.

Teaching required: Teacher facilitates the making of movement phrases. Teacher teaches the choreographic structures. Teacher facilitates and coaches the creation of the dance sections or complete dances. Teacher videotapes the dance and facilitates student self-evaluations and revisions of their dance sections or full dances.

Student Work 4

Students will write and practice connecting oral report sections that link or explain the flight concepts communicated in the dance sections or dances.

Assessment: Oral report sections meet teacher- and student-created rubric based on district or national standards. Oral report notes are turned in as portfolio evidence.

Teaching required: Teacher may have to teach strategies for oral reports.

Refinement Task: Allowing for Revision

Since the premise of this book is "the process is the process," look at table I.1, Comparison of Cognitive Processes (page 2). The refinement task, across all four of the processes, calls for peer evaluation and self-evaluation. At any time during the project design process, you (and your team) should share the written draft of the integrated project with an outsider, someone who has not been involved with the project. Let that person read and critique the document. He or she should ask you clarifying questions about your goals for each aspect of the project. From this critique, you should be able to make any necessary revisions.

No matter how much experience you have in designing and implementing integrated work, you will likely have many critiques and revisions before completing integrated projects. As an example, when designing the rubrics for written pieces of student work, you will find it helpful to ask another teacher to critique your rubrics for clarity.

Students, like everyone else, learn through completing multiple drafts of their work. The revision of student work is an essential part of the creative process and allows for opportunities to refine and make changes as needed before the final product is presented. Peer assessment, self-assessment, and teacher assessment can provide students with valuable insight. It is your job to design activities and allow time for such revision.

Student Work 6

Revisions on lecture/demonstrations are based on self-evaluations and peer evaluations.

Assessment: Revisions are videotaped for the students' portfolio evidence.

Teaching required: Teacher facilitates students' revision process.

Exhibition Task: Performing Completed Work and Accepting Final Critique

As part of a real-world application, students should perform in a public sharing. Students will rise to the occasion when given the opportunity to share their work with a real audience. The exhibition or culminating event not only raises the stakes of the student work by adding external pressure, but it also serves as a celebration of the student work. Examples of this are the public performance of the dance or theater production, an oral presentation, and a public display of a report. This task is used for identifying performance opportunities as well as how the performance will be assessed and documented. Performance opportunities are plentiful within a community. From performing at the local preschool to presenting student work before a jury of professionals, public exhibitions have relevant and lasting effects on student learning.

The audience's reaction to, and evaluation of, the exhibition function as feedback. Student evaluations, self-evaluations, and peer evaluations give more insight on the success of the project. The student work itself, collected in a process portfolio and graded by the final rubric, also provides clear feedback. It is up to you and your students to reflect on and learn from both the successes and the shortcomings of the integrated project.

The following example of exhibition is found in the Flight Integrated Project.

Once you have planned your integrated project, use form 7.1, Template for Integrated Projects (included on the CD-ROM), to formally write up the project. This is when you fill in all the specific

Exhibition raises the stakes for all involved.

details as demonstrated by the three complete integrated projects that are included in this book. The structure design includes an overview of the project (project title, content areas addressed, focusing or guiding question, rationale for the project, major piece of student work, exhibition or culminating event) followed by a sequence of student tasks. Each of the student tasks provides the following information: title, description of student work, standards to be met, student instructions, rubric, and portfolio evidence. These sections are directed at the student and can be transferred directly to form I.1, Student Work Form, on the CD-ROM. On form 7.1 these sections are followed by teaching required, materials needed, and suggested time frame, which are directed to you and provide what you need to enable the students to complete the work successfully. This process may seem complicated at first, but once you've experienced the excitement of your colleagues, students, and audiences, you will be rewarded with a feeling of satisfaction and pride in what your students have learned.

Student Work 7: Exhibition or Culminating Event

Students present lecture/demonstrations to an audience of students, teachers, and special guests. (Special guests could be aeronautics or aviary experts.)

Assessment: Using the rubrics, audience evaluates lecture/demonstrations. (For these rubrics, see forms 10.4 and 10.8.) The final rubric is used for assessing the student work completed over the course of the whole project.

Final Rubric for the Whole Project

(+):

- Student completes all tasks of the project with enthusiasm and attention to detail.
- Portfolio evidence is completed with at least 75% of the work at above standard.
- Student takes part in the lecture/demonstration and workshops.
- Student demonstrates a high quality of reflection in final evaluation process.
- At least 75% of self-, peer, audience, and teacher evaluations are graded at above standard.
- Student volunteers to take on responsibilities beyond what is required.

(✓):

- All tasks of the project are completed.
- Portfolio evidence is completed at standard.
- Student takes part in lecture/demonstration and workshops.

(–):

- Only 75% of the tasks of the project are completed.
- Portfolio evidence is incomplete and/or includes work that is below standard.
- Student participates in only one part of the lecture/demonstration or does not participate in all of the activities.

Table 7.1 Flight Integrated Project As It Relates to Tasks of Choreographic Process

Task	Integrated project
Concept task: choosing a topic	Project Title: Come Fly With Me Standards to be met: dance, physical science, English language arts (specific to states and grades). Major piece of student work: Students will create a grade-appropriate lecture/demonstration that explains, with the help of dance, one of the following concepts: the power of air, overcoming gravity, laws of motion, forces of flight (lift, propulsion, weight, and drag), how birds fly, and wing function and structure. See grade-specific examples of how birds fly (grades K to 4), forces of flight (grades 5 to 8), and Newton's law of motion (grades 9 to 12).
Investigation task: researching the topic	Research the appropriate topic for grade level. Use form 2.2, List of Research Resources, to help you identify resources to write and for your students' use during implementation.
Exploration task: narrowing the focus	Focusing or guiding question: How can we show the concept of flight through an integrated dance project?
Selection task: designing rigorous student work	In the Flight Integrated Project the major piece of student work is a lecture/demonstration. Student Work 5: Major piece of student work: Using both the dance sections and the oral report sections, students put their lecture/demonstrations together. Assessment: Lecture/demonstrations are videotaped for self-evaluations and peer evaluations. The rubric for the lecture/demonstrations is created by you and the students and is based on physical science, English language arts, and dance standards. Teaching required: Teacher will facilitate the creation of the rubric. Teacher will make suggestions, as needed, for the best organization for the delivery of the lecture/demonstrations.

(continued)

Table 7.1 *(continued)*

Task	Integrated project
Development task: breaking down the learning	Design smaller pieces of student work:
	Student Work 1: In small groups, students research their grade-appropriate topic.
	Assessment: Students hand in note cards or form 2.3, Sources and Notes, for portfolio evidence.
	Teaching required: Teacher gathers research materials and/or bookmarks appropriate Web sites. Teacher instructs students in research strategies.
	Student Work 2: Students do the Flight Inspiration Activity in one class period.
	See Flight Inspiration Activity for grades K to 4 (table 3.2).
	See Flight Inspiration Activity for grades 5 to 8 (table 3.3).
	See Flight Inspiration Activity for grades 9 to 12 (table 3.4).
	Assessment: Students produce movement phrases that demonstrate an understanding of the concept of flight.
	Teaching required: Teacher facilitates the inspiration activity.
	Student Work 3: Students do the Flight Dance Designing Activity in three or four class periods.
	See Flight Dance Designing Activity (Grades K to 4, table 6.1).
	See Flight Dance Designing Activity (Grades 5 to 8, table 6.2).
	See Flight Dance Designing Activity (Grades 9 to 12, table 6.3).
	Assessment: Movement problems (in the dance designing activity) are solved according to the instructions to make a dance section or a complete dance on flight. Students should critique each other on how well the movement problems were solved.
	Teaching required: Teacher facilitates the making of movement phrases. Teacher teaches the choreographic structures. Teacher facilitates and coaches the creation of the dance sections or complete dances. Teacher videotapes the dance and facilitates student self-evaluations and revisions of their dance sections or dances.
	Student Work 4: Students will write and practice connecting oral report sections that link or explain the flight concepts communicated in the dance sections or dances.
	Assessment: Oral report sections meet teacher- and student-created rubric based on district or national standards. Notes on oral reports are turned in as portfolio evidence.
	Teaching required: Teacher may have to teach strategies for oral reports.

Refinement task: allowing for revisions	Get feedback from colleagues and other people. Use this feedback to develop and revise your integrated project.
	Also make sure that you design opportunities for students to develop and revise their work.
	The Flight Integrated Project provides students with opportunity for revision.
	Student Work 6: Revisions on lecture/demonstrations based on self-evaluations and peer evaluations (see forms 10.8 and 10.9).
	Assessment: Revisions are videotaped for the students' portfolio evidence.
	Teaching required: Teacher facilitates students' revision process.
Exhibition task: performing completed work and accepting final critique	Design your exhibition or culminating event and assessments:
	Student Work 7: exhibition or culminating event:
	Students present lecture/demonstrations to an audience of students, teachers, and special guests. (Special guests could be aeronautics or aviary experts.)
	Assessment: Using the rubrics, audience evaluates lecture/demonstrations. (For these rubrics, see forms 10.4 and 10.10.)
	The final rubric is used for assessing the student work completed over the course of the whole project.
	Final rubric for the whole project:
	(+): • Student completes all tasks of the project with enthusiasm and attention to detail. • Portfolio evidence is completed with at least 75% of the work at above standard. • Student takes part in the lecture/demonstration and workshops. • Student demonstrates a high quality of reflection in final evaluation process. • At least 75% of self-, peer, audience, and teacher evaluations are graded at above standard. • Student volunteers to take on responsibilities above and beyond what is required.
	(✓): • All tasks of the project are completed. • Portfolio evidence is completed at standard. • Student takes part in lecture/demonstration and workshops.

(continued)

Table 7.1 *(continued)*

Task	Integrated project
	(–): • Only 75% of the tasks of the project are completed. • Portfolio evidence is incomplete and/or includes work that is below standard. • Student participates in only one part of the lecture/demonstration or does not participate in all of the activities. You should implement your integrated project. Use student work, grades, portfolios, and final critiques to improve your abilities in planning and implementing future integrated projects.

Chapter 8

Moving the Project Forward: A Time Line

Mounting a theatrical production requires planning, teamwork, and use of a time line so that everyone completes his or her part of the performance on schedule. Implementing an integrated project is much the same as putting on a theatrical production: It is like solving a puzzle. Of course, the work of carrying out a project can be undertaken by one person. However, it is so much easier and so much more fun when you assemble a team of people to work with you. With a project and end date in mind, you can use the information in this chapter to help you solve the puzzle of what to do and when. You can adjust the schedule to suit the needs of your school. The time line and the tasks involved are adaptable. Needed changes can be made on the spot. It is a work in progress. The time line and tasks can be used as a template for future integrated projects.

Please note that chapters 7 and 8 should be read in tandem. Chapter 7 deals with creating and writing an integrated project, and chapter 8 deals with the practical aspects of creating and implementing the project. You must consider two components when creating, writing, and implementing an integrated project. The first component is the actual creating and writing of the integrated project. In chapter 7 it is assumed that you alone are wholly responsible for writing the project; however, as you just read, this can be done as a team. The second component is the actual production of a product. We are dance educators who mostly deal with mounting dance productions, but this process can also be applied to any type of exhibition, such as a formal debate, forum, or an art exhibit.

Making Connections: Where to Go for Help

You should consider three major areas of resources when creating and implementing integrated dance projects. One of these resources is project team members, including teachers, students, and community members. The second source of help to consider is the research resources available. This involves more resources than an encyclopedia reference. Finally, you need to find funding for your project. If the school budget doesn't include funds for integrated projects, then you will have to search elsewhere.

Building the Team: The People Connection

The collaboration always produces more than the sum of the individual contributions—that is, synergy. In *Dance About Anything,* dance functions as the cement holding together the subject areas as well as the teams of teachers and students. Each of the individuals (teachers and students) brings a particular strength to the team. The teaching team members could include dance educators, physical educators, classroom teachers, visual art educators, music educators, theater educators, resource teachers, industrial arts teachers, and home and consumer science teachers. In addition to the teachers and students, the teaching team could include students' family members, professional artists, local community members with specific expertise on the idea of the project, and anyone else interested in supporting the teaching and learning. All teachers are responsible for honing critical- and creative-thinking skills, providing the content, contributing research skills and knowledge, and encouraging the physical nature of the dance activities.

An integrated project is a team project, and you can act as the team captain. As that captain, you can use all the help you can get! You should see crossovers into many academic disciplines. For writing a story or script, an English teacher would be helpful.

Teachers can cross over discipline lines during integrated projects. Science teachers can create visual art and all teachers can create movement.

That person would also be very helpful in reading and interpreting written research material. When it comes to the making of scenery and props, the industrial arts teacher is a strong ally. For the making of costumes, the services and knowledge of the home and consumer science teacher would be a perfect resource. A social studies teacher would be able to help with map making and demographics (what facts are known about a specific population). A science teacher might be the one to help sort out any topographical or ecological aspects needed for a project geared to the sciences, such as flight or weather. The media specialist at school or within the community will have much-needed information on where and how to find research materials. Of course, any teacher in the school with a flare for theatrics and for bringing a subject to life will be excited about being part of such a project. Don't forget that certain people in the community can be valuable players on your team. Depending on your topic, you can call on the weather forecaster, people from other countries, historians, authors, artists from all genres, and local celebrities. Talk to them about your ideas and the enthusiasm of the students. Ask for their input on the project. Praise their abilities and their passions. Tell them how you and the students can use their expertise.

Again, the question remains of how to get people involved. At this point, the project is in written form. You either initiated the inspiration, or the integration team came up with the inspiration together. The latter method surely would get the team involved from the start. Either way works well.

Students bring the energy, excitement, imagination, enthusiasm, and sense of play to the project. Their enthusiasm will motivate everyone involved, and their energy can keep the momentum going. A personal touch can be very effective. Speak to someone with whom you work well. The key to success is to start small. Work with just one or two other teachers. The first time you may only want to ask them for a small favor—what expertise can they offer?

After you have a handle on the process of team building and team teaching, you can expand your team to include more faculty members. Another way to begin to recruit a team is to invite several colleagues to coffee or lunch or an after-school treat. You know your colleagues. What would appeal to them? Do your homework and lay out the project in the most exciting fashion. The more enthusiastic you are, the more you will engage them. Be confident in the knowledge that you can make this work. When others see your excitement and success and the intensive learning that takes place, they will come to you to ask how they can become involved and help.

Once you have all your colleagues together, you can either ask for their help in specific areas, come up with ideas on the main topic and what they would like to see included, or ask what part of the project is of most interest to them. You can share with them the ideas students shared with you, and together you can prioritize and organize. Be ready to relinquish some of the power that goes with being a lone creator. Embrace their ideas as you did the students' ideas. As with the students, the more input they have, the more they will want to continue to be involved. This buy-in is important.

You will also want to inform your administrator about the project and the goals. Gaining support from the top is a big plus. The timing and the way you introduce the project are up to you. You certainly want the support and enthusiasm of the administrative staff. Be sure to explain the benefits of working within the school community and neighborhood community.

Digging for Information: Research Resources

You need to get your resources in place so that your students and fellow teammates have a place to start. Many of these items have been mentioned as the project was being designed; however, when looking at the time line for the entire project, we think it needs to be included here as well. We all have used libraries as traditional ways to do research. Now we have the Internet at our disposal. This has an upside and a downside. You need to tell your students to verify their Internet sources. We have found that some of the materials found on the Web are just people's opinions, sites disappear and reappear at random, and it is difficult to determine credibility and sources of certain sites.

Interviews with experts are an important aspect of research. You can set up these interviews so that the expert comes to your school. The students can plan to do this as a group, or individual students can have a specified amount of time with the guest. Don't be afraid to do this part of the process with young students. They usually ask the most pertinent questions without fear of embarrassment.

Finding Funding: How Deep Is the Well?

When you gather your team, one of the first things you need to address is funding. Many school systems do have money in their

Students are also experts and can help teach.

Teaching artists from your community can add to your integrated project.

budgets for planning and implementing a project that would include so many teachers and students. However, many school systems have no funds at all. You have to start with two budgets. One will be the high-end budget and the other will be the bare-bones budget. Keep the two lists side by side. Some of the expenses will remain the same for both. Items on your lists should include space rental (if any); cost of music selections; recording costs; paper supplies (if not available through the school); costumes (either for raw materials like fabric, notions, and thread or for already-constructed costumes); and scenery and prop supplies. Don't forget that you may have to pay theater technicians for their services. You may need to compensate members of your team, as well. Contact people in the school system and from the community to see if they have items that you can borrow.

You have borrowed and created much of what the project requires, but you still need cash. You can establish an ongoing sale of some food items during lunches. We have seen people fund their programs and projects with sales of ice cream, nachos, candy, and flowers for special occasions (Valentine's Day, Mother's Day, Easter, Thanksgiving). All this takes planning, but the students can do the selling and adult volunteers can make the contacts to obtain the goods.

For some, the step of fund-raising is the most frightening, but if you don't ask, people won't give. And remember, people give to people, not to causes, so go to your friends and associates first. The easiest way to build up your account is to go to local banks, businesses, police and fire departments, and civic organizations (Lions Club, Rotary, and Knights of Columbus to name a few). Be brave and proud of your work. Call first and ask about their sphere of giving. Ask to speak to the person in charge of community relations. That person might just send you some information. When you see even a remote match, write a letter explaining your project and why it is important. Make a connection between what you are doing and how the business or civic group can help. Offer them a listing in the program book. About a week after you send the letter, follow up with a phone call and ask for an appointment. You don't have to do this alone. This is another case in which the team approach works. Watch for plaques on walls of businesses that support sport teams and music programs. That is a good lead into asking them for money to support your students and their unique efforts. A picture from past performances and some old programs also go a long way in establishing your credibility. A letter from your principal will be equally helpful. Just remember that success breeds success; once you get some funding, you can tell the other people you go to that you are already getting support from another local source. Won't you be thrilled to be able to proceed with your higher budget?

Time Line of Process

Selected text adapted, by permission, from H. Scheff, M. Sprague, and S. McGreevy-Nichols, 2005, *Experiencing dance: From student to dance artist* (Champaign, IL: Human Kinetics), 141-144.

Following is a list of responsibilities and a logical order for fulfilling them. This information can serve as a template for organizing an implementation schedule for your semester-long integrated dance project. We lead you through a week-by-week breakdown of jobs, based on an 18-week semester, but you can easily adapt this structure to your specific needs. See table 8.1 for a summary of this information in a time-line format. Within our weekly descriptions, you will find what each job entails. Do not forget your postperformance tasks at the end of the schedule! Note that when implementing the integrated project, you will find that members of the team from other subject areas may change places with you. You all will be interchangeable but will act as a team.

Table 8.1 Time Line of Tasks to Be Completed for Integrated Dance Projects

Week	Task
Week 1	• Book performance space. • Name project director. • Assess technical needs based on meeting during project design stage.
Week 3	• With your support team of students and colleagues, gather strategies to deal with technical needs.
Ongoing	• Rehearse. • Revise. • Reflect.
Week 12	• Launch publicity campaign. • Send invitation letters. • Send parent letters.
Week 14	• Collect materials for inclusion in souvenir program book.
Week 15	• Revisit technical needs. • Make changes to accommodate funds and abilities. • Arrange for backstage help during performance.
Week 16	• Arrange for ticket sales. • Arrange for help at front of house.
Final week before performance	• Handle performance-week flurries. • Run technical and dress rehearsals. • Do last-minute costume, scenery, and prop checks.

Adapted from H. Scheff, M. Sprague, and S. McGreevy-Nichols, 2005, *Experiencing dance: From student to dance artist* (Champaign, IL: Human Kinetics), 141-144.

Week 1

At the beginning of the project, you need to secure a performance space. You also need to name a project director; for our purposes, that person is you. Meet with your technical support staff, whether they are paid or volunteer, to discuss what kinds of help you need and in what order. You might need set pieces first so that your performers learn to move around them. You might decide on dealing with issues of special lighting, such as the illumination of a door or window frame for a special entrance.

As you work at finding a performance space, consider the following issues. The amount of stage space is important to many of the decisions you will make. The performance space you use could be the school auditorium, the cafetorium (multipurpose room), a recreation center with a stage, a community theater, or even a community meeting place. Make sure that you and the people who usually use the space are clear on the dates. Mark calendars and, where necessary, sign agreements. Of course, in an ideal world you would get the space free of charge, but if it is a community facility you might offer the revenue from one of the performances in lieu of paying a rental fee.

Week 3

With your team and the students, think of the technical needs of the production: scenery, costumes, props, sound, lighting, and extras (such as a fog or smoke

Anna Leonowens' dress for Anna and the King.

Props can complete a production.

machine). Make lists of your needs. *This should happen a few weeks into the project.* Once you have your ideas, prioritize them so that you will know ahead of time what you can afford and how much time you have to devote to making these things happen.

For our project on Anna and the King, Anna needs a huge, billowing ball gown. If you have the cash and a staff to build a costume like that, then by all means take the time and money to make it. But if money, staff, and time constraints are considerations, you can make do with a borrowed costume or drape fabric over a hoop. The industrial arts teacher or home and consumer science teacher can help with the manufacturing of the hoop and skirt, and the visual arts teacher can help with the costume design and special trimming. They, in turn, can enlist the aid of their students. Of course, the student work (researching the period fashion and how it should be used) is an element of the project. A similar process takes place with scenery, lights, props, and extras.

Ongoing Jobs and Responsibilities: Rehearse and Revise

As soon as research has been developed and the guiding statements and questions have been asked, the ongoing job of rehearsing and revising can begin. The entire point of an integrated project is that it is developed from student work with facilitation by the teacher. The reading, research, and problem solving evolve into the substance of the project. For instance, as choreography is developed, it also needs to be refined. This happens by revision and reflection. Revision happens with peer evaluation, self-evaluation, and teacher evaluation. You will find sample evaluation forms on the CD-ROM (see forms 5.1 and 5.2). Reflection happens when you look at a particular part of the project to see how close it is to the original intent. The hardest part here is knowing when to stop the revision process—knowing when changes are being made just for the sake of changing something and not for improving the project.

Week 12

Most publicity campaigns fall short of success because there is a notion that it can all come together at the last minute. The importance of publicity is to inform. You want as many people to know about the final performance as possible. A minimum of six weeks before the performance, complete the following tasks to devise your publicity campaign:

1. **Send letters of invitation to target audiences.** The letter should include where, when, what, why, and who, known as the five Ws. If the target audience is invited guests, you should include that fact, or a complimentary ticket should accompany the letter. If the audience is expected to pay, then the price of admission should be included in the letter. This letter could go to school groups for block booking of the performances. **Block booking** means that several schools within a district come to the show, or several classes within a school come to the same performance. Groups that block-book should pay a reduced admission fee.

2. **Send public service announcements to the local media.** Again, include the five Ws. A call to these people for their format requirements (how they like to receive information), time frame, and deadlines is most helpful in getting them to air your message. In many media areas, they want the information a full month ahead. Some need to know only two weeks ahead, whereas the public service announcements and requests for coverage on radio and TV are better received the week of the show. Sometimes they give you an absolute deadline and, conversely, the earliest time you can submit information. *The week of the performance, send faxes to the local TV stations.* This notification would be for the purpose of covering the performance and not for advance publicity.

3. **Write, call, or fax the newspapers.** You, or whoever is handling publicity, might be able to get them to arrange an interview with the students or you for a feature print article.

4. **Write letters to parents.** This letter announcing the event would also have a permission slip attached if any of the performances were to take place at a time other than the school day or at a site other than your school.

Week 14

About a month before the performance, you should start collecting materials for your souvenir program. This would include the order of the performance, names of the performers, the teachers involved in the project, the choreographers, names of all the people who helped (some with a special thank-you), and names of the technical crew. You will want a cover design with pertinent information included on the cover, such as time, date, location, title, and admission price (if applicable). You might also want to include a written note or paragraph about the development of the piece. For instance, for Anna and the King, the subject of culture clash is the basis of the project. You would write a paragraph outlining this fact. For the Community Quilt, you would include in the program a paragraph detailing the process of learning about the community. You can make revisions to the program on the computer up until the last week. Determine the amount of time you need for the programs to be ready for the performance. This will depend on whether you decide to use the services of a professional printing firm or if your school can print the programs.

Week 15

At the very beginning of the process, you met with the technicians. You also need to do this during the course of planning the production and then again at a minimum of three weeks before the performance. The first meetings have to do with needs and

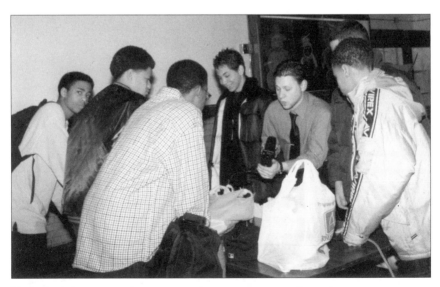

Technical theater students can make your props and set pieces.

wants. The meetings three weeks before the event are when you will assess what has been accomplished and what still needs to be done. It is also a time when you will begin to use props and set pieces with your performers because it is unfair to ask your performers to incorporate the use of props and set pieces during the week of the show. Secure enough backstage help for costume and scenery changes as well as light and sound-board operators. Everyone (and that includes performers) needs to understand back-stage behavior and etiquette. These behaviors can be discussed at a full-cast meeting.

Week 16

About two weeks before the performance, you should arrange for tickets and ticket sales. You can have students design a ticket on the computer. The ticket should include the name of the per-formance, the date and time of the performance, the place, the admission fee, and who is presenting. If there are performances on several different dates and times, and the public is invited, the date and time on the ticket should be changed for each perfor-mance. You can sell tickets ahead of time, or you can limit sales to tickets at the door. You will need some very responsible people to sell and collect tickets. Even if you do only door sales, you need to have patrons' tickets so that you can cross-check the numbers of people against the cash collected. Here is another place where team members who are not performing can help.

Final Week: Technical Rehearsal and Performance

The time has come to put together all the work and set it in its final stage. You should schedule a technical rehearsal before the performers get on stage. This is when the light crew, scene crew, sound crew, costume crew, and prop crew refine what they have to do in order to make the show run. A stage manager has the final say on when the curtain goes up. You need to make technical information sheets for each dance, which list anything special that would concern the technical crew. They can then run a **cue-to-cue rehearsal** without the dancers. This means that the rehearsal involves running the music, sound, curtain, and light cues from the beginning of the show to the final curtain. Then the dancers should be added to the mix. Even if the performance space is not a stage but a gym, multipurpose room, or cafetorium, this technical rehearsal should take place. It makes the dress rehearsal run much more efficiently.

When you get to the dress rehearsal, *don't panic.* The performers will be excited. Don't expect everything to run smoothly. You will have expectations that are not being met, but remaining calm is of utmost importance. Students will be scrambling for missing costume pieces or props, insisting that it isn't where they put it. The narration doesn't fit into the space in the music. The flashlights for the torches are not working as expected. What to do?

You or your student stage manager should make a list of the problems. Some crewmembers can solve the problems if given direction in an instructive manner. Others problems can be solved between rehearsals, and some may not be solvable. Yelling and blaming get you nowhere. A calm, clear, and controlled approach will get the jobs done that can be done. Some things you will just have to let go.

The night of the performance has arrived. Your participating students arrive one hour before performance time. You have enlisted the aid of colleagues or parents to take ticket money and check tickets. You have students who will usher. This is not a big deal if you haven't sold numbered seating. At a general admission show, you need helpers only to give out the programs. Your front-of-house staff will also greet special guests. If you have invited other schoolchildren, then you will need the ushers to escort the guest classes to their assigned rows. Make sure you have the seating capacity for those who have been invited. Fifteen minutes before showtime, check on the performers and stage crews to be sure everything is in place. Everyone has done his or her job, and a semester's worth of work is about to be showcased.

As if by magic, it all pulls together, and the cheers and applause from the audience put smiles on the faces of the performers and technicians alike. Your team is exhilarated, and everyone involved in the project is in the winner's circle. The warm glow continues through multiple performances, and there is some sadness when everyone realizes that it is all over.

Postperformance Tasks

All that is left to do is to **strike** (break down or take apart) the show. That means that cast and crew carefully store costumes, scenery, and props with the hope of recycling them into other projects. Thank-you notes should be written and sent to the appropriate people. Make a folder of all the resources used and collected for the project (a school archive). This could include designs, construction records, light plots, programs, sample tickets, reviews, evaluation notes, names, and contacts for people who helped with the project as well as any financial information such as expenses and income. A postperformance team meeting, sometimes called a postmortem, is a good idea. This is where you can list the highs and lows of the project while it is still fresh in everyone's mind. This may also be a good time to plant the seeds of creativity for the next project.

Roles and Responsibilities

It is difficult to divide the responsibility. You don't want people to think that they are being overworked. Sometimes you will find that what you are teaching is not entirely your subject of record, but it is an area where you have a level of expertise.

List of Roles and Responsibilities for Any Integrated Project

1. *Teachers* collect and become familiar with the materials that will be used to enhance student learning and the project.
2. *Teachers* choose dates, times, and place for the final exhibition or performance.
3. *Teachers* devise a reading guide and a viewing guide for the students to help them become more familiar with the topics. If available, a video for the youngest groups of children would be most appropriate. For students in middle school, you could have the books on hand from which they could glean important facts. For the upper-level students, you could send them to libraries and research sites to find information.
4. *Students* do research either from a selected list or from what they come up with on their own. They list the ideas they wish to communicate on the topic. As noted earlier, younger students will need more direction, and older students should be expected to do some independent research.

(continued)

(continued)

5. *Students* can prioritize ideas that will affect and interact with the theme.

6. *Students* begin to explore movements that convey their ideas.

7. *Teachers,* with possible *student* input, choose music.

8. *Teachers* facilitate the students' joining of movements into phrases and dances.

9. *Students, teachers,* and *adult volunteers* design costumes, props, scenery, and lights. In a perfect world, you will be able to incorporate all of the elements mentioned. Students have vast imaginations. They can be the ones to inspire the ideas for costumes, props, scenery, and lights.

10. *Students, teachers,* and *adult volunteers* construct costumes, props, scenery, and light plots. The students can do the sewing and gluing. They can also help paint scenery and props.

11. *Students* and *teachers* write a script or narration. (With this step, the dances can be placed in an appropriate order.)

12. *Students, teachers,* and *adult volunteers* send invitations and write and send press releases. Fliers are designed and distributed and tickets are sold. When you are doing a project with younger grade levels, use the skills they have. Who could resist an invitation with some third-graders' artwork on the front?

13. *Teachers* put together the production as the final pieces of a puzzle. The teachers meet with other adult team members to finalize the script and the order of the show. The students are then notified of the order and any changes from the original format.

14. It is showtime. When a stage manager is in charge of keeping the performance on track, he or she would say, "Places, everyone. Showtime!" just before the curtain rises. If there isn't a curtain, this command would become a light cue (such as flashing the lights) so that both the audience and the performers would be aware that the show is about to start.

15. After the performance is over, *teachers* and *students* strike (take apart) the show by putting everything away. The term *strike* has nothing to do with hitting anything; rather, it involves deconstructing the sets and storing props and costumes.

16. Final evaluations are written by *all concerned* with the project. Each member of the team should list comments germane to the project. The details of what transpired are important to future works.

17. *Students* and *teachers* write and send thank-yous to appropriate people. Those getting thank-you notes from the students will be deeply touched.

Preperformance Audience Activity Booklet

When you invite other schools to view the performance of your integrated dance project, it is often beneficial for them to have some knowledge of the story line. It is even more fun for your students (in both dance and other curricula) to create the activities that will be included in the booklet. The process of creating the booklet is simple, and you and your project teammates can work together with your students. You should send this booklet to schools when they confirm that they will attend the performance. Ask your students to sign their contributions; this work can become part of their portfolios.

Meet with students involved in the integrated project and presentation. Together, think about the project and what you want audience members to know before they come to the show. Analyze the grade levels of your invited audiences and design your activity books accordingly. Plan to make two activity books, one for the lower grades and one for the upper grades. The following are suggested features to include in the books:

- A cover page that denotes some important aspect of the show (such as a main character, an important piece of scenery, or the title and location of the presentation)
- A simple story line geared to the targeted age levels
- The cast of characters and their relationships to one another (you might even add how the characters will be dressed to aid the audience in identifying characters)
- The order of the scenes and which characters will appear in them and what is to happen during the scene (the running order of the show would be the template for this information)

- For audience members in the upper grades, a character analysis of the main characters written by your students to help the audience better understand why some things happen as they do
- Any supporting material such as the music being used and how and where to find it
- An evaluation form to be filled out after the performance
- A postperformance questionnaire on the audience's new knowledge

Now for the fun part! Select some activities from the following ideas:

- Word searches
- Crossword puzzles
- Characters or scenes to be colored
- Mazes to find a character or an object
- Cross-matches—matching character names with relationships or attributes
- Project-specific crafts, such as a pattern for a fan with an Asian theme, instructions for making a tom-tom for a Native American theme, or flag patterns for a project with an international theme
- A page for a written or illustrated personal reaction to listening to a piece of music from the show
- Anything your students think of that would be interesting for the audience to know and to do before viewing the show

Show the students examples of simple, commercially-made activity books. This might inspire them to create different pages. We have included a sample booklet in the appendix section of the CD-ROM for your reference. Please note that the art in our sample booklet was drawn by a professional illustrator. The art in your booklet should be drawn by students.

Being a Good Audience Member: Know How to Act During a Formal Performance

Being a good audience member means different things to different people and different situations. At a sporting event, hoots and hollers are expected. The players even use the audience noise to get pumped up. A rock concert also calls for hoots, shouting, and singing with the performers. However, patrons at dance concerts, orchestral or jazz concerts, plays, and operas have a different set of expected behaviors. Tell your students to think about the following recommendations for being a good audience member the next time they go to a theater to view a performance of any kind:

1. Follow the common courtesy of getting to the performance and being seated on time.
2. Do not talk to your neighbors during the performance. You can talk to them before or after the performance.
3. Pay attention to what is happening in the performance.
4. Listen to or watch the performers. It is part of your job as an audience member.
5. Applause is expected at the end of the performance. Loud and thunderous applause is appropriate for something you really enjoyed. Soft, polite applause is appropriate for something that was not your favorite.
6. Whistling is out of the question. Refrain from such behavior.
7. Do not use flash photography because it is dangerous to performers and annoying to fellow audience members.
8. In some instances (such as at opera and dance performances), applause is expected after a particular section of the performance. Pay attention to those around you; they will give you clues about when to acknowledge the performers.
9. Standing ovations should be reserved for the end of a performance when you are truly overjoyed at what you saw and heard.
10. Turn off all cell phones and beepers when you walk into the theater space. Do not turn them back on until you exit.

(continued)

(continued)

11. Refrain from eating during the performance. Noisy candy wrappers and the popping of gum disturb your fellow audience members.

12. Yelling is not acceptable. Audience members may shout, "Bravo!" after a particularly exciting piece of work. This is done while seated or when standing for an ovation.

13. You may make notes while enjoying the performance for the purposes of recording your observations. No electronic recording devices of any kind are permitted in the performance space.

14. Viewing a performance is very different from watching something on television. You can't "pause" and go off to get something to eat or drink, go to the bathroom, or make a phone call. Please take care of these things before you enter the theater or at intermission.

By following these recommendations, you will have done your part to make the theater experience the best it can be for you, your fellow audience members, and the rest of the audience.

Chapter 9

Sparking Students' Interest: Effective Teaching, Facilitating, and Coaching

It is always difficult to maintain anyone's interest during a long project. Attention may wander and energy may wane. One way of ensuring that your students stay engaged in integrated projects is to assume various roles during the learning and teaching process: teacher, facilitator, and coach.

Selecting the Appropriate Teaching Style

As a student moves from the first hesitant contact with new content of the new product or learning (through your use of direct teaching), through the hands-on manipulation of skills and concepts (through your use of facilitating), and finally through the assessment, revision, and exhibition (through your use of coaching), you need to provide different types and amounts of support. This use of different teaching roles is like the age-old method of imparting knowledge and skills called apprenticeship. During an apprenticeship, a master artisan first teaches the skills and concepts necessary to the craft, then steps back and facilitates the student's efforts, offering a helpful cue or reminder. Finally the master artisan casts a critical eye on the student's work, or evaluates, and coaches the student through the production of a better, revised piece of work.

All effective learning requires the use of a variety of teaching styles. The type of work that a student is asked to do determines the most effective style of teaching. Three teaching styles that are used in integrated projects are **direct teaching, facilitating,** and **coaching.** For the purposes of this book, we use the following descriptions of direct teaching, facilitating, and coaching as we use them in our teaching and learning activities. All three styles are essential in successful instruction. While reading the following descriptions, consider who is primarily responsible for the student learning.

Direct Teaching

In this style of direct teaching, you, the teacher, have knowledge or information that is imparted directly to the student. In direct teaching, you instruct, the student learns, and then you test the student's learning. Direct teaching actually starts when you develop the student work and assessments that cover the curriculum and meet national and local standards. You should act as the overall development manager. This management includes planning the projects and lessons. These projects and lessons should take into account students' prior learning and the new knowledge that the students need in order to complete their work. Direct teaching should occur when there is a gap in the students' knowledge or skill that prevents them from completing an assignment. This is a valid mode of instruction when used strategically throughout the project. In this book, direct teaching is necessary in the dance designing activities and in parts of the integrated projects.

For example, the students create two dance phrases and decide they like one phrase more than the other, but they still want to use both. You suggest that they organize their dance phrases into an ABA choreographic structure. You then should resort to direct teaching of the ABA choreographic structure. We have used the image of a sandwich. A is one dance phrase followed by B, a contrasting dance phrase, followed by A, the repeat of the first dance phrase. This analogy refers to a slice of bread, the filling, and the other slice of bread. The students are now ready to continue with their dance making.

Facilitating

Facilitating requires that you step back from the lead in the teaching and learning process. Guiding, prompting, and encouraging are the main instructional activities of this teaching style. Here the students take on more responsibility for their work. Students are working on student assignments, and the doing is synonymous with the learning. The facilitator helps the students focus on their work through cues and prompts and by arranging an environment conducive to creativity and good work. You, as facilitator, can aid students in following the guidelines and can assist students that need help in applying their knowledge to the work. This assistance is also necessary for students who need to develop more self-management and teamwork skills. Leading and guiding discussions are facilitating skills. In assessment, the job of the facilitator takes on two forms. As facilitator, you can help students evaluate their own work. You can also make suggestions so that students can develop their own assessments. (This development of assessment should be done before the students engage in the work.) When students are involved in developing their own criteria and rubrics, they take ownership of their learning process. The work improves.

For example, in the inspiration activities presented in this book, you provide the materials necessary for the activities and then step back. The students are allowed to figure out on their own what the clue and the description mean and then create their movement. You should step in only when students need a bit of prompting, reassurance, or gentle reminders of what effective teamwork is. Also during the revision and exhibition stages, you are present to provide a safe environment for the sharing of movement phrases. If you have taught students how to respectfully observe and critique other students' work, then a meaningful look, gesture, or clearing of your throat will suffice as facilitation strategies if a student's behavior goes astray.

Coaching

Coaching is vital in the final revision and rehearsal stage. At this point in the teaching and learning process, students must deliver evidence of their work. They need the confidence to display their work before an audience. A coach, having an idea of the quality of the work that the students should produce, stands back, observes, and critiques students for clarity in their performance. The coach makes suggestions for improvement in student work and devises small assignments that can improve performance. One important requirement is to encourage repetition and practice. As a coach, your job is to prepare the student for independence. You should step back to cheer and encourage from the sidelines. You must allow the students to demonstrate their learning on their own.

For example, the students have completed their dance, but they perform it with major hesitations between sections of their dance. You, as coach, should inform the students of these hesitations and help them rehearse the transitions between the dance sections.

Combining Direct Teaching, Facilitating, and Coaching

Following are examples of how and when direct teaching (T), facilitating (F), and coaching (C) are employed in inspiration activities, dance designing activities, and integrated projects.

During the inspiration activity, you function mainly as a facilitator. The formula is only F; another possible formula could be F + T + F.

- F: Facilitate the creation of the inspiration movement phrase.
- T: Teach the skills required for improvement.
- F: Facilitate the revision process and sharing session.

During the dance designing activity, you employ all three teaching styles. The formula is T + T/F + F + (T + C).

- T: Design learning activities and teach necessary skills and knowledge.
- T/F: Design assessment *or* facilitate student-designed assessment.
- F: Facilitate students engaging in the creative process.
- (T+C): Teach and coach in order to prepare students for revision and exhibition.

During integrated projects, instruction can flow seamlessly from style to style as needed. You must be ready to use any style in order to keep the work on track and on the highest level. The formula is T + T/F + F + T + F + (T + C) + T.

- T: Design learning activities and teach necessary skills and knowledge.
- T/F: Design assessment *or* facilitate student-designed assessment.
- F: Facilitate as students engage in the creative process.
- T: Give more needed skills and knowledge.
- F: Facilitate as students engage in the creative process.
- (T + C): Teach and coach in order to prepare students for revision and exhibition.
- T: Design next project as the assessment shows student needs or gaps.

Once you are knowledgeable of the three styles of teaching, you will be able to choose whichever style is needed. Because you are not directing their every move, students will have ownership of their work, thereby ensuring interest.

Chapter 10

Evaluating Integrated Projects: The Big Picture

The student learning that occurs throughout the implementation of the integrated dance project is far more than what is identified within specific standards for subject content. Integrated projects afford students the opportunity to work through a problem; create a plan; evaluate and revise their work; collaborate as a team; research, analyze, and process information; and perform as if in real-world situations. In fact, through their involvement in integrated projects, students acquire skills and knowledge that are valued by the larger community, especially the business community.

Identifying Workforce Skills

The Secretary's Commission on Achieving Necessary Skills (SCANS) was appointed by the U.S. Secretary of Labor to determine the skills young people in the United States need in order to succeed in the workforce. In 1991, SCANS issued their initial report, *What Work Requires of Schools*. One of the goals of this report is to help teachers understand how curriculum and instruction need to change to enable students to develop the skills for success in the workplace. Table 10.1, SCANS-Identified Workforce Skills, summarizes the skills, knowledge, and dispositions that are identified in this report.

Table 10.1 SCANS-Identified Workforce Skills

Thinking skills	Personal qualities	Resources	Interpersonal	Information	Systems	Technology
Individual thinks creatively, makes decisions, solves problems, visualizes, knows how to learn, and reasons.	Individual displays responsibility, self-esteem, sociability, self-management, and integrity and honesty.	Individual identifies, organizes, plans, and allocates resources.	Individual works with others.	Individual acquires and uses information.	Individual understands complex relationships.	Individual works with a variety of technologies.
Creative thinking: Generates new ideas.	*Responsibility:* Exerts a high level of effort and perseveres toward goal attainment.	*Time:* Selects goal-relevant activities, ranks them, allocates time, and prepares and follows schedules.	*Participates as member of a team:* Contributes to group effort.	*Acquires and evaluates information.*	*Understands systems:* Knows how social, organizational, and technological systems work and operates effectively with them.	*Selects technology:* Chooses procedures, tools, or equipment including computers and related technologies.
Decision making: Specifies goals and constraints, generates alternatives, considers risks, and evaluates and chooses best alternative.	*Self-esteem:* Believes in own self-worth and maintains a positive view of self.	*Money:* Uses or prepares budgets, makes forecasts, keeps records, and makes adjustments to meet objectives.	*Teaches others new skills.*	*Organizes and maintains information.*	*Monitors and corrects performance:* Distinguishes trends, predicts effects on systems' operations, diagnoses deviations in systems' performance, and corrects malfunctions.	*Applies technology to task:* Understands overall intent and proper procedures for setup and operation of equipment.

Problem solving: Recognizes problems and devises and implements plan of action.	Sociability: Demonstrates understanding, friendliness, adaptability, and empathy.	Material and facilities: Acquires, stores, allocates, and uses materials or space efficiently.	Serves clients/customers: Works to satisfy customers' expectations.	Interprets and communicates information.	Improves or designs systems: Suggests modifications to existing systems and develops new or alternative systems to improve performance.	Maintains and troubleshoots equipment: Prevents, identifies, or solves problems with equipment, including computers and other technologies.
Seeing things in the mind's eye: Organizes and processes symbols, pictures, graphs, objects, and other information.	Self-management: Assesses self accurately, sets personal goals, monitors progress, and exhibits self-control.	Human resources: Assesses skills and distributes work accordingly, evaluates performance, and provides feedback.	Exercises leadership: Communicates ideas to justify position, persuades and convinces others, responsibly challenges existing procedures and policies.	Uses computers to process information.		
Knowing how to learn: Uses efficient learning techniques to acquire and apply new knowledge and skills.	Integrity and honesty: Chooses ethical courses of action.		Negotiates: Works toward agreements involving exchange of resources, resolves divergent interests.			
Reasoning: Discovers a rule or principle underlying the relationship between two or more objects and applies it when solving a problem.			Works with diversity: Works well with men and women from diverse backgrounds.			

Adapted from Secretary's Commission on Achieving Necessary Skills, 1991, *What work requires of schools.* (Washington, DC: U.S. Department of Labor.)

An integrated project provides students with multiple opportunities to practice and develop many of these identified skills. For example, you might want to assess students' ability to organize themselves throughout the project, follow through with all aspects of the project, accept and use feedback, and work with other students. Use skills from table 10.1 to identify criteria and develop rubrics to assess the various aspects of the project such as teamwork, project management, and nondance presentations as well as to evaluate students' performance throughout the entire implementation of the project. Examples of rubrics that contain these skills are included at the end of this chapter and in the CD-ROM (see forms 10.4-10.7).

Identifying and Assessing Nondance Products

Integrated projects are usually not limited to dance works. They might include a report, oral presentation, or PowerPoint presentation used in conjunction with a lecture/demonstration. They might include large and small exhibitions such as poster displays, learning fairs, student-created museums, and memorials. These types of situations provide perfect opportunities for you to involve other content teachers as advisors and evaluators. Ask these colleagues to help you develop criteria and rubrics, act as jurors, and advise you on critical content and standards. You will be reassured at how much help your fellow faculty members can be. The Internet can also provide rubrics that can help you to evaluate these products. Simply do an Internet search using the key word *rubrics* to locate a multitude of options for rubrics.

Responding to Dance

An integrated project that includes dance also provides opportunities for students to serve in the role of audience member. The process of describing, analyzing, and critiquing their work and that of others provides essential student learning. This same process can be used with professional works as well as with the student pieces.

The responding process can be used as part of the exhibiting task to help assess the student work. Student performances can be assessed by the audience, peers, and teachers as well as by self-evaluations. Evaluations by all of these give a complete picture of student work. Videotaping is essential for documentation, as a means of evaluating, and as a tool to be used for planning future integrated projects. On the CD-ROM, evaluation forms are included to help with these tasks (see forms 10.8, 10.9, and 10.10).

Creating a Process Portfolio

An integrated project involves students in complex thinking and decision making. It involves students in the development and production of rigorous student work that meets multiple standards in multiple disciplines. It is important to document all aspects of the student work, including student thinking and the steps students take to complete the work. We have found that a **process portfolio** is an effective tool for documenting student work. A process portfolio can be used for everything from a single work to projects completed over the course of a school year. When completed, the portfolio will reveal a complete picture of the students' learning. There are many options for documentation: checklists; journal entries; worksheets; peer, teacher, and self-evaluations; video; audio; and still photography. As we mentioned in the introduction, when using video and photography in your classroom, a video and photography release form (signed by students' parents or guardians) may be necessary. Check with your principal for your school's rule on this matter. The various worksheets included in this book are particularly useful in pulling together an effective process portfolio. Managing the portfolio can be made easier by using checklists that identify the overall contents. Enlist your students in keeping track of portfolio items and recording grades for the various pieces. If you have a computer with a scanner and CD-burning capacity, you can even help students develop electronic portfolios.

Using the Worksheets to Assess the Big Picture of Integrated Projects

Use the following assessment forms to help you and your students revise, evaluate, and analyze student work throughout the implementation of the integrated unit.

- **Form 10.1, Integrated Project Checklist:** Use this form as part of the process portfolio to keep track of the completion of student tasks within the integrated project.

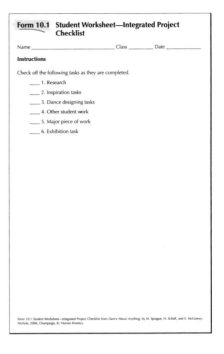

Form 10.1 Student Worksheet—Integrated Project Checklist

Name _____ Class _____ Date _____

Instructions

Check off the following tasks as they are completed.

_____ 1. Research

_____ 2. Inspiration tasks

_____ 3. Dance designing tasks

_____ 4. Other student work

_____ 5. Major piece of work

_____ 6. Exhibition task

Form 10.1 Student Worksheet—Integrated Project Checklist from *Dance About Anything*, by M. Sprague, H. Scheff, and S. McGreevy-Nichols, 2006, Champaign, IL: Human Kinetics.

- **Form 10.2, Student Work Form:** Use this form for the individual pieces of student work. This form focuses students on project criteria and standards met, and it provides clear instructions and a rubric for assessing the work. This form also doubles as a cover sheet for the student work.

Form 10.2 Student Worksheet—Student Work Form

Name _____ Class _____ Date _____ Student work #_____

Description of Student Work
Students will do the following:

The work will include the following:

: _____

: _____

Standards Met

Student Instructions

1. _____

2. _____

3. _____

Rubric

Portfolio Evidence

Form 10.2 Student Worksheet—Student Work Form from *Dance About Anything* by M. Sprague, H. Scheff, and S. McGreevy-Nichols, 2006, Champaign, IL: Human Kinetics.

- **Form 10.3, Journal Entry Portfolio Sheet:** Students can use this form at any point in the process to reflect on learning. Also have students use this form to focus on and answer specific questions that may come up throughout the project.

Form 10.3 Student Worksheet—Journal Entry Portfolio Sheet

Name _____ Class _____ Date _____

Instructions
Write the assigned question and your response in the appropriate spaces.

Focusing and reflective question:

Response:

Form 10.3 Student Worksheet—Journal Entry Portfolio Sheet from *Dance About Anything* by M. Sprague, H. Scheff, and S. McGreevy-Nichols, 2006, Champaign, IL: Human Kinetics.

- **Form 10.4, Oral Presentation Checklist:** Use this form to assist students with perfecting oral presentations. You and your students can also use the form as an assessment tool to evaluate oral presentations.

Form 10.4 Student Worksheet—Oral Presentation Checklist

Name _____ Class _____ Date _____

Instructions
Use the following scale to rate the presenter: (+) above standard, (✓) at standard, or (–) missing any at-standard criteria.

For a presentation that is at standard, the oral presenter should do the following:

_____ Make movements or gestures that enhance presentation.
_____ Use direct eye contact with the audience.
_____ Use clear introductory and closing remarks.
_____ Effectively pace his or her words.
_____ Appear confident, make minimal mistakes, and be able to continue with the presentation.
_____ Be clear and loud enough to be understood.
_____ Use notes in an effective, nondetracting way.
_____ Use content that meets the class-generated criteria.

For a presentation that is above standard, the oral presenter should do the following:

_____ Demonstrate all the previous criteria.
_____ Use effective audio or visual aids to enhance the presentation.
_____ Deliver the presentation with a great deal of personality.

Form 10.4 Student Worksheet—Oral Presentation Checklist from *Dance About Anything* by M. Sprague, H. Scheff, and S. McGreevy-Nichols, 2006, Champaign, IL: Human Kinetics.

- **Form 10.5, Evaluation of Teamwork:** This form can be used at many points throughout the implementation of the integrated project. Use the form as a self-evaluation, as a peer evaluation, and as a teacher evaluation of students' contribution to the team effort.

Form 10.5   Student Worksheet—Evaluation of Teamwork

Name _____ Class _____ Date _____

Instructions

1. Use the following rubric to evaluate one of these two aspects:
   a. _____ My teamwork
   b. _____ The teamwork of a peer
   Name of peer _____
2. Total the points from the last column and place the total score in the box at the bottom.

Teamwork skills	1: None of the time	2: Some of the time	3: Most of the time	4: All of the time	Points
Offers assistance to others.					
Listens to the ideas of others.					
Contributes to the group work.					
Exchanges, defends, and rethinks ideas.					
Poses and discusses questions with the team.					
Encourages and supports the ideas and efforts of other team members.					
Offers to perform additional tasks and reports findings to the team.					
Assumes a leadership role.					

25 to 32 = above standard
17 to 24 = at standard
0 to 16 = needs improvement

Total points:

Form 10.5 Student Worksheet—Evaluation of Teamwork from *Dance About Anything* by M. Sprague, H. Scheff, and S. McGreevy-Nichols, 2006, Champaign, IL: Human Kinetics.

- **Form 10.6, Evaluation of Project Management:** This form directly relates to those skills that are identified in the SCANS. Use this form to evaluate students' ability to accomplish specific skills throughout the implementation of the integrated project.

Form 10.6   Student Worksheet—Evaluation of Project Management

Name _____ Class _____ Date _____

Instructions

1. Using the following scoring guide, rate the person on overall project management.
2. Total the points from the last column and place the total score in the box at the bottom.

	1: Not evident	2: Sometimes	3: Most of the time	4: Always	Points
Understands and contributes to the project.					
Has a clear vision of the entire project.					
Is properly organized to complete project.					
Manages time wisely.					
Acquires needed knowledge base.					
Checks in with teacher or leader as required.					
Completes required work on time.					
Responsibility, self-esteem, sociability, integrity.					
Exerts a high level of effort.					
Maintains a positive view of self and others.					
Demonstrates understanding, friendliness, adaptability, and empathy.					
Assesses accuracy, sets personal goals, monitors progress, and exhibits self-control.					
Sticks with a task until completed in spite of distractions.					
Acquires, evaluates, organizes, and uses information.					

(continued)

Form 10.6 Student Worksheet—Evaluation of Project Management from *Dance About Anything* by M. Sprague, H. Scheff, and S. McGreevy-Nichols, 2006, Champaign, IL: Human Kinetics.

- **Form 10.7, Evaluation of Thinking Skills:** This form can be used at many points throughout the implementation of the integrated project. Use the form as a self-evaluation, as a peer evaluation, and as a teacher evaluation of students' thinking skills.

Form 10.7 Student Worksheet—Evaluation of Thinking Skills

Name _____ Class _____ Date _____

Instructions
Discuss where you have used the following skills during the integrated project. Use specific examples.

Creative Thinking
Generates new ideas.
Example 1:

Example 2:

Example 3:

Decision Making
Specifies goals and constraints, generates alternatives, considers risks, and evaluates and chooses best alternative.
Example 1:

Example 2:

Example 3:

Problem Solving
Recognizes problems and devises and implements plan of action.
Example 1:

Example 2:

Example 3:

(continued)

Form 10.7 Student Worksheet—Evaluation of Thinking Skills from *Dance About Anything* by M. Sprague, H. Scheff, and S. McGreevy-Nichols, 2006, Champaign, IL: Human Kinetics.

- **Form 10.8, Perform Your Final Product and Evaluate Its Success:** This form assesses students' understanding of what makes a good performance, dance vocabulary, and their understanding of the revision process as a way to improve choreography.

Form 10.8 Student Worksheet—Exhibiting Integrated Projects: Perform Your Final Product and Evaluate Its Success

Name _____ Class _____ Date _____

Instructions
Do the activities and answer the questions.

1. Work on your performance or presentation. Think about what makes a good performance or presentation. Use the following space to note these ideas and why you think they are important. (You and your teacher can use your answer to create a rubric for your performance or presentation.)

2. Perform or make your presentation for your peers. Ask them for further ideas on revisions to make your performance stronger. Try to incorporate these ideas and revise the presentation as necessary. List some of the suggestions from peers. Explain how you will use the suggestions to make the quality of your exhibition better.

Form 10.8 Student Worksheet—Exhibiting Integrated Projects: Perform Your Final Product and Evaluate Its Success from *Dance About Anything* by M. Sprague, H. Scheff, and S. McGreevy-Nichols, 2006, Champaign, IL: Human Kinetics.

- **Form 10.9, Responding to Dance As Part of an Integrated Project:** Students use this form when responding to dance. Any piece of choreography created by either professionals or students or performed live or on tape can be used. This form challenges all levels of thinking.

- **Form 10.10, Audience Worksheet—Evaluation of Project:** This form is used by the audience to evaluate the final project and student performance as part of that project.

Form 10.9 Student Worksheet—Responding to Dance As Part of an Integrated Project

Name _____ Class _____ Date _____

1. Select a piece of work (a dance).
   - Title of dance: _____
   - Title of integrated project: _____

2. Describe the work in detail. (What is the topic, idea, theme, or inspiration?) Describe, where applicable, the general movements, costumes, props, music, scenery, and lighting.

3. Analyze (categorize, study, discover). Describe elements, choreographic structures, formations, composition, and organization.

4. Interpret (decode, predict, explain). Describe your impressions of the dance. What do you think the performer meant to portray? What were the moods, feelings, and images you saw and felt?

5. Evaluate (critique, assess, inquire). What is your opinion of the piece and why? Support your opinion using details and examples from items 3 and 4.

6. How did this dance piece bring together parts of the integrated project?

Form 10.9 Student Worksheet—Responding to Dance As Part of an Integrated Project from *Dance About Anything* by M. Sprague, H. Scheff, and S. McGreevy-Nichols, 2006, Champaign, IL: Human Kinetics.

Form 10.10 Audience Worksheet—Evaluation of Project

Description of Project

Assessment Criteria

1. Did the dance pieces convey the idea, topic, or story as described? Briefly explain why or why not.

2. Describe a part in the dance that you thought was particularly interesting or effectively performed. Briefly explain why.

3. Using a scale from 1 (needs improvement) to 5 (excellent), how would you rate the quality of the student performance?

Other comments:

I am a(n) (check all that apply)

   parent _____
   student _____
   invited guest _____
   teacher _____
   administrator _____
   community member _____
   performer _____

Form 10.10 Audience Worksheet—Evaluation of Project from *Dance About Anything* by M. Sprague, H. Scheff, and S. McGreevy-Nichols, 2006, Champaign, IL: Human Kinetics.

Summary of Part III

In chapter 7, we define what constitutes an integrated project and walk you through the process of creating and writing one. Chapters 8 and 9 provide practical information on implementing a successful integrated dance project. Chapter 10 focuses on the integrated project as a whole and discusses some of the valuable life and work skills that can be learned as part of an integrated project. This chapter also assists you in evaluating the total project, providing you with evaluation forms that can be used as part of a process portfolio.

Part IV

Three Complete Themes and Integrated Projects

You are now ready to implement an integrated project. Part IV is divided into three chapters, and each chapter is a full integrated project. Although we have designated a project for each set of grade levels, there is no reason that you cannot adapt each one to your students' needs and ability levels by adding deeper material or by doing more direct teaching than coaching and facilitating.

The first project is in chapter 11, Cosmic Influences: Weather You Like It or Not (grades K to 4). Although you can implement this project on your own, it provides an opportunity to use people in your school community and the community at large to make up your team. Science teachers, media teachers, and the men and women on your local radio and TV stations that deliver the weather reports can all be involved. Often even local printed media have a page for weather, and in some areas this page is geared to children.

The next project is in chapter 12, Community: Community Quilt (grades 5 to 8). This project addresses the issues surrounding diverse communities where one neighbor doesn't know the other or knows very little about the different ethnic heritages that make up the neighborhood. The product—the quilt—and the celebration that ensues bring all the facts and people together. The children learn about one another and learn to respect one another from interviewing community members (business owners, their employees, and residents).

The final project is in chapter 13, Prejudice and Human Rights: Anna and the King (grades 9 to 12). This subject matter engages English language arts teachers, history teachers, and social studies teachers. Prejudice is an issue that is not unfamiliar to any particular country or time in history. People involved in this project should come away with a new light on how prejudice and lack of human respect can bring very hard and sad times to a small community or to nations.

You have been given three complete projects. The planning and outlining have been done for you. What a perfect opportunity to discover the exciting learning that takes place and how willing the students are to contribute, which in turn will give them the pride of ownership.

Chapter 11

Cosmic Influences:
Weather You
Like It or Not
(Grades K to 4)

APPROPRIATE GRADE LEVEL

Kindergarten to Grade 4.

CONTENT AREAS ADDRESSED

Dance, science, English language arts.

FOCUSING OR GUIDING QUESTION

How can we show scientific concepts of weather through dance?

PROJECT RATIONALE

People watch weather forecasts all the time without knowing exactly what causes weather conditions.

MAJOR PIECE OF STUDENT WORK

Students create a lecture/demonstration that explains, with the help of dance, selected weather concepts, such as cold and warm fronts, depressions, thunder and lightning, wind, and the tides and weather.

EXHIBITION OR CULMINATING EVENT

Students present their lecture/demonstration to peers; younger students, such as students in lower grades and day care; parents; and special guests, such as guest speakers who visited during the project or the local weather person.

Student Work 1: Inspiration Activity

Description of Student Work

 Students explore the Weather Inspiration Activity (form 3.8). The work includes creating a short movement phrase.

Standards Met

- Science (Earth and space)
- English language arts (writing, reading, and viewing)
- Dance (dance as communication; critical and creative thinking)

Student Instructions

1. Students read and follow the instructions on the Weather Inspiration Activity Card (form 3.8).
2. Students' movement phrases are videotaped.

Rubric

Students create a short movement phrase. No rubric is necessary. Teacher or students check off completion of work on form 11.1, Integrated Project Checklist: Weather (shown at the end of the chapter and included on the CD-ROM).

Portfolio Evidence

- Videotape of movement phrase
- Form 11.1, Integrated Project Checklist: Weather

Teaching Required

- Facilitate the Weather Inspiration Activity (form 3.8).
- Videotape movement phrases.
- Review the entire integrated project using form 11.1, Integrated Project Checklist: Weather.

Materials Needed

- Form 3.8, Inspiration Activity Card: Weather
- Form 11.1, Integrated Project Checklist: Weather
- Blank index cards
- Assorted resource books on weather
- List of Web resources on specific weather topics or copies of excerpts from Internet resources
- Video camera and blank tape

Suggested Time Frame

Two class periods.

Student Work 2: Research Activity

Description of Student Work

Students research assigned topics relating to weather. The work will include evidence of research (note cards and forms 2.1 and 2.3).

Standards Met

- Science (Earth and space)
- English language arts (writing, reading, and viewing)

Student Instructions

1. In small groups, students select and research one of the following topics:
   - Clouds
   - Fronts (cold and warm)
   - Jet steams
   - Cyclones, tornadoes, hurricanes, monsoons
   - El Niño
   - Air masses
   - Seasons
   - Temperature
   - Storms
   - Precipitation
   - Depressions
   - Thunder and lightning
   - Wind
   - Tides and weather

2. Students complete a note card for each clear point or idea found in their research concerning their selected topic.

3. Students should record the source of the information, author, page number, Web site (if applicable), and year of publication. For example, "The windchill factor is a number often expressed as an equivalent temperature, that expresses the cooling effect of moving air at different temperatures" (Lyons, 1997, p. 205).

Rubric

Students hand in documented evidence of research. Teacher or students check off completion of work on form 11.1, Integrated Project Checklist: Weather.

- Above standard (+): Student has 11 or more cards per topic.
- At standard (✓): Student has 5 to 10 cards per topic.

Note: You may wish to use form 2.3, Sources and Notes, instead of note cards.

Portfolio Evidence

- Note cards
- Form 11.1, Integrated Project Checklist: Weather

Teaching Required

- Gather research materials or bookmark appropriate Web sites.
- Review with students form 2.2, List of Research Resources.
- Instruct students on proper citation of research sources. Refer to form 2.4, Bibliography Reference Sheet.

Materials Needed

- Form 2.2, List of Research Resources
- Form 2.3, Sources and Notes
- Form 2.4, Bibliography Reference Sheet
- Form 11.1, Integrated Project Checklist: Weather
- Blank note cards
- Assorted resource books on weather
- List of Web resources on specific weather topics or copies of excerpts from Internet resources

Suggested Time Frame

Three class periods.

Student Work 3: Exploring the Topic

Description of Student Work

Students identify words, phrases, and ideas from research that best suggest movement. The work will include completed worksheets.

Standards Met

- Science (Earth and space)
- English language arts (writing, reading, and viewing)

Student Instructions

1. Students review the research (note cards) that they have completed on their topics.
2. Students use form 3.1, Using Visualization to Select Text for Movement, to identify words and phrases that will help them in creating **moving images.**

Rubric

Teacher or students check off completion of work on form 11.1, Integrated Project Checklist: Weather.

- Above standard (+): Student completes 4 or more worksheets.
- At standard (✓): Student completes 2 or 3 worksheets.

Portfolio Evidence

- Worksheets
- Form 11.1, Integrated Project Checklist: Weather

Teaching Required

- Help students identify the words, phrases, and ideas that best suggest movement.
- Model how to complete the worksheets.

Materials Needed

- Form 3.1, Using Visualization to Select Text for Movement
- Form 11.1, Integrated Project Checklist: Weather
- Research note cards from Student Work 2

Suggested Time Frame

Two class periods.

Student Work 4: Dance Designing Activity

Description of Student Work

Students create movement problems and movement phrases that explain aspects of their topic. The work will include the following:

- Completed worksheets describing movement problems
- Solutions to movement problems (movement phrases or dance sections)

Standards Met

- Science (Earth and space)
- English language arts (writing, reading, and viewing)
- Dance (choreographic structures, processes, and elements; dance as communication; critical and creative thinking)

Student Instructions

1. Students participate in the Weather Dance Designing Activity (form 6.8). This experience will serve as a model for when they create their own movement phrases based on their selected topics.
2. Students review all the research (note cards) that they have completed on their topics.

3. Students use form 4.4, Designing Movement Problems, to create movement phrases based on specific research facts.
4. Students' completed movement phrases are videotaped.

Rubric

Movement problems are handed in as portfolio evidence. Movement phrases are videotaped for possible revision. Teacher or students check off completion of work on form 11.1, Integrated Project Checklist: Weather.

- Above standard (+): Students create 2 or more movement phrases for each weather concept.
- At standard (✓): Students create at least 1 movement phrase for each weather concept.

Portfolio Evidence

- Worksheets
- Videotape of movement phrases
- Form 11.1, Integrated Project Checklist: Weather

Teaching Required

- Model the dance-making process using the dance designing activity.

- Facilitate the group work and make dance suggestions based on form 4.1, Dance Ideas List, and form 4.4, Designing Movement Problems.

- Videotape the students' completed movement phrases.
- Reference the following student handouts: form 3.3, How to Make Literal Movements Into Abstract Movements; form 4.2, Choreographic Structures Resource Sheet; and form 4.3, Choreographic Processes and Elements Resource Sheet.

Materials Needed

- Form 4.1, Dance Ideas List
- Form 4.4, Designing Movement Problems
- Form 6.8, Dance Designing Activity Card: Weather
- Form 11.1, Integrated Project Checklist: Weather
- Completed research note cards
- Video camera and blank tape; each activity would be recorded on one tape with all students. Individual student work is to be dubbed on their own video later.
- Student handouts:
    - Form 3.3, How to Make Literal Movements Into Abstract Movements
    - Form 4.2, Choreographic Structures Resource Sheet
    - Form 4.3, Choreographic Processes and Elements Resource Sheet

Suggested Time Frame

Six to eight class periods.

Student Work 5: Oral Report

Description of Student Work

Students write and practice connecting oral report sections that link or explain the weather concepts of the movement phrases. The work will include the following:

- Student-generated checklist of criteria for an effective short narration
- Written oral report or narration with presentation note cards

Standards Met

- Science (Earth and space)
- English language arts (writing, reading, and viewing)

Student Instructions

1. Students generate criteria for an effective short narration.
2. Students create pieces of narration that they will use to link the various movement ideas that explain their selected weather concept.
3. Students create note cards that will guide them through the oral part of their lecture/demonstration.
4. Students use the criteria that they generated for short narrations to evaluate the written presentation.

5. Students review form 10.4, Oral Presentation Checklist.
6. Students practice delivering their oral presentations. If possible, these practices will be videotaped.

Rubric

Assessment: Oral report sections meet teacher- and student-generated checklist of criteria for an effective short narration based on district or national standards (see sample criteria in the Teaching Required section). Notes from the oral report are turned in as portfolio evidence. Teacher or students check off completion of work on form 11.1, Integrated Project Checklist: Weather.

Portfolio Evidence

- Written report or presentation note cards
- Videotape of practice presentations
- Student-generated checklist of criteria for an effective short narration
- Form 11.1, Integrated Project Checklist: Weather

Teaching Required

- Discuss with class how to develop and write short narrative "sound bites" that work with the dance to create an effective lecture/demonstration.

- With class, think of criteria for what makes an effective piece of short narrative, and record it on chart paper. (The following are sample criteria: details are factual, content relates to dance movement, content works with the movement to give a complete picture of what is being conveyed.)
- Videotape the practice.
- Review with students form 10.4, Oral Presentation Checklist.

Materials Needed

- Form 10.4, Oral Presentation Checklist
- Form 11.1, Integrated Project Checklist: Weather
- Chart paper and marker
- Video camera and blank tape; each activity would be recorded on one tape with all students. Individual student work is to be dubbed on their own video later.

Suggested Time Frame

Three class periods.

Student Work 6: Major Piece of Work

Description of Student Work

Students create a lecture/demonstration that explains, with the help of dance, selected weather concepts. The work will include the following:

- Oral presentation with note cards
- Movement phrases

Standards Met

- Science (Earth and space)
- English language arts (writing, reading, and viewing)
- Dance (choreographic structures, processes, and elements; dance as communication; critical and creative thinking)

Student Instructions

1. Students combine or sequence their movement phrases with the narrative to create a lecture/demonstration on their selected weather topics.

2. Students practice their lecture/demonstrations.
3. Students' lecture/demonstrations are videotaped.

4. Students view the practice videotapes and complete self-evaluations and peer evaluations using form 10.8, Perform Your Final Product and Evaluate Its Success.

Rubric

Lecture/demonstrations are videotaped for self-evaluations and peer evaluations. The students and teacher create the rubric for the lecture/demonstrations; the rubric is based on district or national standards for science, English language arts, and dance. Teacher or students will check off completion of work on form 11.1, Integrated Project Checklist: Weather.

Portfolio Evidence

- Student-generated rubric designed to evaluate content of lecture/demonstration
- Self-evaluation using form 10.8, Perform Your Final Product and Evaluate Its Success
- Peer evaluation using form 10.8, Perform Your Final Product and Evaluate Its Success
- Practice videotape
- Form 11.1, Integrated Project Checklist: Weather

Teaching Required

- Assist students with their presentations.
- Facilitate creation of criteria or rubric for quality of the content of the final piece of student work. For example, determine at-standard criteria for quality of the dance, quality of the oral presentation, and overall articulation of the weather concept. (See the book's introduction for more information about criteria and rubrics.)
- Help students decide on an order for delivery of all the presentations.
- Make sure all students have a video permission slip on file.
- Videotape students' lecture/demonstrations.

Materials Needed

- Peer evaluation and self-evaluation developed using student-generated criteria to evaluate the quality of the content of the final piece of student work
- Form 10.8, Perform Your Final Product and Evaluate Its Success
- Form 11.1, Integrated Project Checklist: Weather
- Video camera and blank tape; each activity would be recorded on one tape with all students. Individual student work is to be dubbed on their own video later.

Suggested Time Frame

Four class periods.

Student Work 7: Revision of Work

Description of Student Work

Students revise their lecture/demonstrations based on self-evaluations and peer evaluations. The work will include the following:

- A journal entry describing the revisions that were made and why they were made
- A videotape of the students' rehearsal and final product

Standards Met

- Science (Earth and space)
- English language arts (writing, reading, and viewing)
- Dance (dance as communication; critical and creative thinking)

Student Instructions

1. Students review all evaluations.
2. Students discuss feedback with their group and make revisions on lecture/demonstration as needed.

3. Students use form 10.3, Journal Entry Portfolio Sheet, to comment on their revisions.
4. Students' rehearsal and final product are videotaped.

Rubric

Students made revisions on lecture/demonstration and submitted form 10.3, Journal Entry Portfolio Sheet, reflecting on revisions. Teacher or students will check off completion of work on form 11.1, Integrated Project Checklist: Weather. Revisions are videotaped for the students.

Portfolio Evidence

- Videotape of revised lecture/demonstration
- Form 10.3, Journal Entry Portfolio Sheet
- Form 11.1, Integrated Project Checklist: Weather

Teaching Required

- Facilitate students' revision process.
- Assist students as needed with efforts in revision.
- Videotape students' rehearsal and final product.

Materials Needed

- Form 10.3, Journal Entry Portfolio Sheet
- Form 11.1, Integrated Project Checklist: Weather
- Video camera and blank tape; each activity would be recorded on one tape with all students. Individual student work is to be dubbed on their own video later.

Suggested Time Frame

Two class periods.

Student Work 8: Exhibition or Culminating Event

Description of Student Work

Students deliver a lecture/demonstration to an audience of students, teachers, and special guests, such as guest speakers who visited during the project and the local weather person. The work will include final performance evaluations and reflections.

Standards Met

- Science (Earth and space)
- English language arts (writing, reading, and viewing)
- Dance (dance as communication; critical and creative thinking)

Student Instructions

1. Students polish their performance.
2. After the performance, students watch a tape of the performance and complete final evaluations and reflections.

3. Students complete form 10.5, Evaluation of Teamwork, rating their personal efforts and the efforts of a randomly selected person on their team.

Rubric

The following evaluations will be completed:

1. Performance

   • Form 10.8, Perform Your Final Product and Evaluate Its Success (self-evaluation)
   • Form 10.10, Audience Evaluation of Project (audience evaluation)
2. Overall project
   • Form 10.5, Evaluation of Teamwork (self-evaluation and peer evaluation) and evaluation by teacher
   • Reflective essay (an optional self-evaluation): a one-page essay that describes each student's personal involvement in the project; the changes he or she might make in personal efforts during the next project; how the project contributed to personal growth; and how he or she sees the learning transfer to other learning situations

Final Rubric for Entire Project

Above Standard (+)

- Student completes all tasks of the project.
- Portfolio evidence is completed with at least 75% of the work at above standard.
- Student takes part in the lecture/demonstration and workshops.
- Student demonstrates a high quality of reflection in final evaluation process after completing the exhibition.
- At least 75% of the self-, peer, audience, and teacher evaluations of exhibition are graded at above standard.
- Student volunteers to take on responsibilities above and beyond what is required.

At Standard (✓)

- All tasks of the project are completed.
- Portfolio evidence is completed at standard.
- Student takes part in lecture/demonstration and workshops.
- At least 75% of self-, peer, audience, and teacher evaluations are graded at standard.

Portfolio Evidence

- Form 10.5, Evaluation of Teamwork
- Form 10.8, Perform Your Final Product and Evaluate Its Success
- Form 11.1, Integrated Project Checklist: Weather
- Summary of audience evaluations

Teaching Required

- Help students arrange for facilities, invitations, and other site needs. Review chapter 8 to help with these ideas.
- Facilitate the evaluation process, including form 10.10, Audience Evaluation of Project. Prior to this, students drafted brief descriptions that need to be inserted into that form (Description of Project and Assessment Criteria).
- Videotape the performance.

Materials Needed

- Form 10.5, Evaluation of Teamwork
- Form 10.8, Perform Your Final Product and Evaluate Its Success
- Form 10.10, Audience Evaluation of Project
- Form 11.1, Integrated Project Checklist: Weather
- Video camera and blank tape to tape performance
- VCR and TV to watch tape of performance

Suggested Time Frame

Six class periods (includes final preparations, performances, and post-performance evaluations).

Name _____ Class _____ Date _____

Instructions

Check off or have the teacher sign off on the following tasks as you complete them.

_____ 1. Inspiration activity

_____ 2. Research activity

_____ 3. Exploring the topic

_____ 4. Dance designing activity

_____ 5. Oral report

_____ 6. Major piece of work

_____ 7. Revision of work

_____ 8. Exhibition or culminating event

Form 11.1 Student Worksheet—Integrated Project Checklist: Weather (Grades K to 4) from *Dance About Anything* by M. Sprague, H. Scheff, and S. McGreevy-Nichols, 2006, Champaign, IL: Human Kinetics.

Chapter 12

Community: Community Quilt (Grades 5 to 8)

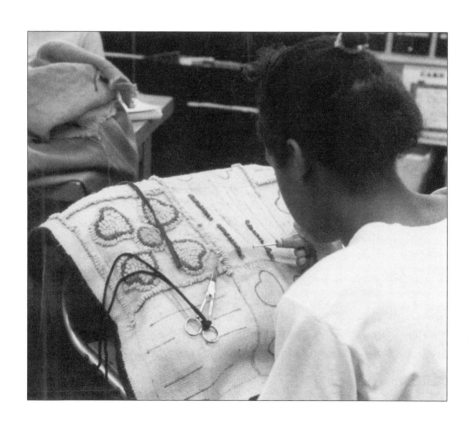

APPROPRIATE GRADE LEVEL

Grades 5 to 8.

CONTENT AREAS ADDRESSED

Dance, social studies, visual arts, English language arts.

FOCUSING OR GUIDING QUESTION

How can we develop a project that will build a sense of community within our neighborhood?

PROJECT RATIONALE

So often, we live our lives without an awareness of other people in our neighborhood. Many people feel isolated. By meeting our neighbors, we can combat this sense of isolation and make our neighborhood a community of people.

MAJOR PIECE OF STUDENT WORK

Students create a quilt, modeled after the fabric artwork of Faith Ringgold. Included in this quilt will be portraits; scenes from the neighborhood; and poems, quotes, and other narrative writing based on interviews with people from the community. Dances will also be created about the community, inspired by aspects found in the quilt.

EXHIBITION OR CULMINATING EVENT

A dedication celebration for the quilt will include dances based on different aspects of this project, favorite foods from the people in the community, and oral readings from the narrative of the quilt and poetic writings.

Student Work 1: Inspiration Activity

Description of Student Work

 Students do the Community Quilt Inspiration Activity (form 3.9). The work will include movement phrases.

Standards Met

- Social studies (cultural influences)
- English language arts (writing)
- Dance (dance as communication and critical and creative thinking)

Student Instructions

1. Students read and carry out the instructions on form 3.9, Inspiration Activity Card: Community Quilt.
2. Students' movement phrases are videotaped.

Rubric

Students create a movement phrase that demonstrates an understanding of the word *community*. A rubric is not required for this piece of work. Teacher or students check off completion of work on form 12.1, Integrated Project Checklist: Community Quilt (shown at the end of the chapter and included on the CD-ROM).

Portfolio Evidence

- Videotape of movement phrase
- Form 12.1, Integrated Project Checklist: Community Quilt

Teaching Required

- Facilitate Community Quilt Inspiration Activity (form 3.9).
- Videotape movement phrases.
- Facilitate a sharing of community dances.
- Facilitate a group thinking session about what the community means to the students.
- Review entire integrated project using form 12.1, Integrated Project Checklist: Community Quilt.

Materials Needed

- Form 3.9, Inspiration Activity Card: Community Quilt
- Form 12.1, Integrated Project Checklist: Community Quilt
- Video camera and blank tape

Suggested Time Frame

Two class periods.

Student Work 2: Dance Designing Activity

Description of Student Work

Students create an original dance using form 6.9, Dance Designing Activity Card: Community Quilt. The work will include the following:

- Copies of interview notes
- A movement or dance phrase that will be combined with those of others.

Standards Met

- Social studies (cultural influences)
- English language arts (writing)
- Dance (choreographic structures, processes, and elements; dance as communication; critical and creative thinking)

Student Instructions

1. Students read through form 6.9, Dance Designing Activity Card: Community Quilt.
2. Students work through the steps of this activity with their assigned groups.

Rubric

- Above standard (+): Both dance design suggestions are completed according to the instructions outlined in the dance designing activity and presented together to make a two-section dance on community.
- At standard (✓): One dance design suggestion is completed according to the instructions outlined in the dance designing activity.

Portfolio Evidence

- Interview notes
- Videotape of movement or dance phrases
- Form 12.1, Integrated Project Checklist: Community Quilt

Teaching Required

- Facilitate the making of movement phrases. Use form 4.4, Designing Movement Problems.
- Reference the following student handouts: form 3.3, How to Make Literal Movements Into Abstract Movements; and form 4.3, Choreographic Processes and Elements Resource Sheet.
- Teach the choreographic structures of rondo and AB.
- Videotape the dances.
- Facilitate student self-evaluation using form 5.1, Evaluating What Works and What Does Not Work, and the revision of their dances.
- Lead the discussion on how the performed dances define the word *community*. Note: These dances will be included in the dedication celebration performance.

Materials Needed

- Form 4.4, Designing Movement Problems
- Form 5.1, Evaluating What Works and What Does Not Work
- Form 6.9, Dance Designing Activity Card: Community Quilt
- Form 12.1, Integrated Project Checklist: Community Quilt
- Student handouts:
  - Form 3.3, How to Make Literal Movements Into Abstract Movements
  - Form 4.3, Choreographic Processes and Elements Resource Sheet
- Video camera and blank tape

Suggested Time Frame

Six class periods.

Student Work 3: Research Activity: Selection of Site

Description of Student Work

Students come up with information about the community and pick a street or part of the neighborhood on which to focus the project. The work will include the following:

- List of suggested items
- Journal entry justifying choice of location

Standards Met

- Social studies (cultural influences; relationship between human actions and environment; migrations; places and regions)
- English language arts (writing)

Student Instructions

1. Students participate in a group thinking session on streets and sections in the neighborhood. Ideas will be recorded on chart paper.
2. Students use form 10.3, Journal Entry Portfolio Sheet, to jot down their thoughts about what location would be the most suitable for the quilt project. They justify their choice by pointing out the historical and cultural significance of the location.

3. Students discuss and defend their choice on why specific sections or streets should be chosen as the focus of the quilt project.

4. Students vote for their favorite location.

Rubric

Students hand in a copy of the information they came up with and their journal entries. Each student votes or participates in the choice of the street or section of the neighborhood. This piece of work does not require a rubric. Teacher or students check off completion of work on form 12.1, Integrated Project Checklist: Community Quilt.

Portfolio Evidence

- List of items from the group thinking session
- Form 10.3, Journal Entry Portfolio Sheet
- Form 12.1, Integrated Project Checklist: Community Quilt

Teaching Required

- Facilitate the group thinking session and record student responses on chart paper.
- Facilitate discussion concerning the best choice of location. Students should justify their choice. (For example, "I think this is a good choice because this is where the Chinese immigrants first settled when they came to this state.")
- Facilitate vote. Count ballots. Announce results.

Materials Needed

- Form 10.3, Journal Entry Portfolio Sheet
- Form 12.1, Integrated Project Checklist: Community Quilt
- Chart paper and marker
- Blank note cards for voting

Suggested Time Frame

Two class periods.

Student Work 4: Research Activity: Development of Questions

Description of Student Work

Students work in teams to create interview questions and an implementation plan for carrying out interviews. The work will include the following:

- List of questions
- Implementation plan

Standards Met

- Social studies (cultural influences; relationship between human actions and environment; migrations; places and regions)
- English language arts (writing, listening, and speaking)

Student Instructions

1. Students discuss the physical, cultural, and historical aspects of the chosen location. These aspects are referenced in local, district, or national geography standards.
2. Students determine what physical aspects are significant, what cultures are represented, and which person or people should be interviewed. These aspects are referenced in local, district, or national geography standards.
3. Students come up with a list of essential information to know about the area.
4. Students draft 10 to 15 interview questions.
5. Students should prepare an implementation plan for the interviews. The plan will include specific interview teams, names of people to be interviewed, proposed schedule for interviews, breakdown of responsibilities, list of materials, and equipment needed.

Rubric

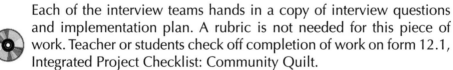

Each of the interview teams hands in a copy of interview questions and implementation plan. A rubric is not needed for this piece of work. Teacher or students check off completion of work on form 12.1, Integrated Project Checklist: Community Quilt.

Portfolio Evidence

- Interview questions
- Implementation plan
- Form 12.1, Integrated Project Checklist: Community Quilt

Teaching Required

- Facilitate a class discussion about the types of information that would be valuable to know when conducting interviews, such as what type of person best represents the selected location, what categories of people exist in the area, what cultures are represented in the area, how people came to live or work there, and the ratio of business to residential buildings.

- Explain what information needs to be in the implementation plan (such as interview teams, schedule of interviews, and breakdown of responsibilities).
- Instruct students on proper etiquette for interviews.

Materials Needed

- Form 12.1, Integrated Project Checklist: Community Quilt

Suggested Time Frame

Two class periods.

Student Work 5: Research Activity: Documentation of Interviewees and Site

Description of Student Work

Through the use of drawings or still photography, students document the storefronts, parks, landmarks, and people to be interviewed. The work will include the following:

- Photos and drawings
- A note card for each photo or drawing documenting details about the image, such as name of person, location of building, and background information.

Standards Met

- Visual art (structures and function, media, techniques, and processes)

Student Instructions

1. With the help of the teacher, students gain written permission from the various people to be photographed.
2. Students should schedule and carry out the various photo sessions.
3. Students fill out a note card on each photo, noting the pertinent information such as name of person, location of building, and background information.

Rubric

Photographs and drawings and note cards are filed in portfolio. A rubric is not needed for this piece of work. Teacher or students check off completion of work on form 12.1, Integrated Project Checklist: Community Quilt.

Portfolio Evidence

- Note cards
- Photos and drawings
- Form 12.1, Integrated Project Checklist: Community Quilt

Teaching Required

- Assist students with gaining written permissions for the photography.
- Provide a small lesson on effective photography. (Collaborate with the visual arts teacher or do an Internet search using key words *elements of photography*).
- Review what information needs to be placed on note cards.
- Review students' schedules.

Materials Needed

- Cameras
- Drawing pads
- Note cards
- Form 12.1, Integrated Project Checklist: Community Quilt

Suggested Time Frame

Two weeks.

Student Work 6: Conducting Interviews

Description of Student Work

Students conduct the interviews; document interviews using audiotape, videotape, or note taking; organize notes or transcribe (write word for word) tape of interviews; and write a short biography on a person, a narrative on a place, or original poem based on the interviewee or location. The work will include the following:

- Notes or tapes (audio or video) of interviews
- Organization and transcription of notes or tapes
- Short biography, narration, or original poem

Standards Met

- English language arts (writing, reading, listening and speaking, viewing, media)

Student Instructions

1. Students conduct practice interviews on classmates and become familiar with any equipment being used.
2. Students conduct interviews and organize or transcribe notes or tapes.
3. Students write up a short biography or create an original poem about the person interviewed.

Rubric

Students submit all required items of the work as described. The work does not need a rubric. Teacher or students check off completion of work on form 12.1, Integrated Project Checklist: Community Quilt.

Portfolio Evidence

- Notes, videotapes, and audiotapes
- Organized or transcribed notes or tapes
- Short biography or poem
- Form 12.1, Integrated Project Checklist: Community Quilt

Teaching Required

- Organize practice interviews.
- Oversee distribution of equipment.
- Discuss how to effectively organize notes and how to listen to tapes and transcribe the contents with accuracy.
- Share models of poems and short biographies; discuss key aspects of both styles of writing. If needed, get help from fellow faculty or do an Internet search using key words *writing poems, short bios,* and *narrations.*

Materials Needed

- Audio or video player and recorder
- Clipboards for note taking
- Audiotapes or videotapes
- Models of poems and biographies
- Form 12.1, Integrated Project Checklist: Community Quilt

Suggested Time Frame

Two weeks.

Student Work 7: Major Piece of Work (Quilt)

Description of Student Work

Students create a quilt (from quilt squares) modeled after the fabric artwork of Faith Ringgold. The work will include quilt squares that portray portraits; scenes from the neighborhood; and poems, quotes, and other narrative writing based on interviews with people from the community.

Note: A parent or some other community volunteer can assemble the quilt with organizational and compositional input from the students. Fusible (iron-on) fabric is also effective for constructing the quilt squares. These quilts hang on the wall. They are not meant to be used as bedding. The quilt can also be created from paper instead of from fabric.

Standards Met

- Visual arts (structures and functions, media, techniques, and processes)
- English language arts (writing, reading, listening and speaking, viewing, media)
- Social studies (cultural influences)

Student Instructions

1. Students create a draft drawing of a quilt square. A poem, narration, or words that pertain to the person, building, or landmark should be included.
2. Students create their final quilt square using designated material (fabric or paper).

3. Teacher works with the class arranging squares to produce a final design. On a larger piece of fabric or paper, squares should be temporarily secured with straight pins (if quilt is made of fabric) or removable sticky material (if quilt is made of paper). A designated person (parent, art teacher, or community member) can assemble the final quilt.

Rubric

Above Standard (+)

- The work is modeled after Faith Ringgold's work and includes a one-page written essay that discusses how this quilt is similar to Ringgold's.
- The quilt represents the community.
- It includes written text.
- It is supported by portfolio evidence from Student Work 1 to 6.

At Standard (✓)

- The quilt represents the community.
- It includes written text.
- It is supported by portfolio evidence from Student Work 1 to 6.

Portfolio Evidence

- Draft of quilt square
- Form 12.1, Integrated Project Checklist: Community Quilt

Teaching Required

- Introduce the students to the work of Faith Ringgold. The students can use the following book as a reference for research: Ringgold, F., Freeman, L., & Roucher, N. (1996). *Talking to Faith Ringgold.* New York: Crown Books. ISBN 0517885478.
- See the following Web sites for information about the artist and some examples of her work:
  - www.ndoylefineart.com/ringgold.html
  - http://falcon.jmu.edu/~ramseyil/ringgold.htm
  - www.pbs.org/americaquilts/century/stories/faith_ringgold.html
- Cut the quilt squares. Gather the rest of the art supplies to be used. Facilitate the composition of the quilt.

Materials Needed

- Fabric and assorted art materials (fabric paint or waterproof markers in an assortment of colors; scissors; accent items such as beads, buttons, small pieces of ribbon or lace)
- Photos or drawings of a variety of quilts
- Photos or drawings of some of Faith Ringgold's quilts
- Copies of *Talking to Faith Ringgold* or other background information on Faith Ringgold
- Form 12.1, Integrated Project Checklist: Community Quilt

Suggested Time Frame

Two weeks.

Student Work 8: Major Piece of Work (Dance)

Description of Student Work

Students create original dances about the community. The work will include original movement phrases created to reflect aspects of the written work, the photographs, and other aspects found in the quilt.

Standards Met

- English language arts (writing, research, reading, listening and speaking, viewing, media)
- Dance (choreographic structures, processes, and elements; dance as communication; critical and creative thinking)
- Social studies (cultural influences)

Student Instructions

1. Students choose aspects from the quilt to use as inspiration for their dance and review narrations and poems.
2. Students review the steps of form 6.9, Dance Designing Activity Card: Community Quilt.
3. Students use the same process that they used for Student Work 2, Dance Designing Activity Card: Community Quilt (form 6.9), to create dances that represent the selected community. Use form 4.4, Designing Movement Problems, to assist in creating movement problems and movement solutions or phrases and designing dances.

4. Students may consider using any of the following additional suggestions for dance designs:

- Create a sound score with sound from the neighborhood and words or phrases from the interview. Use the sound score as an inspiration for a dance.
- Create a dance from the lines, colors, rhythms, shapes, and patterns found in the quilt.
- Create a carnival processional dance with separate sections that represent key characteristics of the community or neighborhood (use theme dances instead of creating traditional theme parade floats).

5. Students' work is videotaped.

Rubric

Above Standard (+)

- Student completed form 4.4, Designing Movement Problems.
- Student evaluated and revised dance.
- Movement phrases are videotaped.
- Dance demonstrates an understanding of the community.
- Dance incorporates one of the additional dance designing suggestions.

At Standard (✓)

- Student completed form 4.4, Designing Movement Problems.
- Student evaluated and revised dance.
- Movement phrases are videotaped.
- Dance demonstrates an understanding of the community.

Portfolio Evidence

- Videotape of movement or dance phrases
- Form 4.4, Designing Movement Problems

- Form 5.1, Evaluating What Works and What Does Not Work
- Form 12.1, Integrated Project Checklist: Community Quilt

Teaching Required

- Review process used in form 6.9, Dance Designing Activity Card: Community Quilt.

- Provide form 4.4, Designing Movement Problems, to assist in the dance-making process.
- Reference the following student handouts: form 3.3, How to Make Literal Movements Into Abstract Movements; and form 4.3, Choreographic Processes and Elements Resource Sheet.
- Facilitate the creation of dances.
- Facilitate revision of the dances. Have students evaluate and revise work with the assistance of form 5.1, Evaluating What Works and What Does Not Work.
- Videotape the dances and place videotape in portfolio.

Materials Needed

- Form 3.3, How to Make Literal Movements Into Abstract Movements
- Form 4.3, Choreographic Processes and Elements Resource Sheet
- Form 4.4, Designing Movement Problems
- Form 5.1, Evaluating What Works and What Does Not Work
- Form 6.9, Community Quilt Dance Designing Activity
- Form 12.1, Integrated Project Checklist: Community Quilt
- Video camera and blank tapes

Suggested Time Frame

Two to four weeks.

Student Work 9: Exhibition or Culminating Event

Description of Student Work

Students plan and host a dedication celebration for the Community of People Quilt. The work will include the following:

- Formal dedication and unveiling
- Dance performances (quilt-inspired dance and Community Quilt Dance Designing Activity)
- Poetry readings and biographies

Standards Met

- Dance (performance of movement elements and skills; choreographic structures, processes, and elements; dance as communication; critical and creative thinking)
- English language arts (writing, research, reading, viewing)
- Visual arts (media, techniques and processes, structures and functions)

Student Instructions

1. Students prepare a list of guests to be invited.
2. Students create an invitation and send it out.
3. Students plan a schedule of events to occur during the dedication ceremony.
4. Students practice and ensure performance pieces (poetry or biographical readings and dances) are as polished as possible.
5. After the event, students watch videotape and complete final evaluations and reflections. The following forms will be used:

   - Form 10.5, Evaluation of Teamwork (self and peer)
   - Form 10.6, Evaluation of Project Management (self)
   - Form 10.8, Perform Your Final Product and Evaluate Its Success (self)

Rubric

Above Standard (+)

- Student completes all tasks of the project.
- Portfolio evidence (including self-evaluation, peer evaluation, and teacher evaluation) is completed with at least 75% of the work rated at above standard.
- Student takes part in the final performance and celebration.
- Student demonstrates a high quality of reflection in the final evaluation process. Student submits a reflective essay that describes personal involvement in the project, what changes the student might make in personal efforts during the next project, and how the project contributed to personal growth.
- Student volunteers to take on responsibilities above and beyond what is required.

At Standard (✓)

- All tasks of the project are completed.
- Portfolio evidence (including self-evaluation, peer evaluation, and teacher evaluation) are graded at standard.
- Student takes part in final performance and celebration.

Portfolio Evidence

- Video of dedication event
- Form 10.5, Evaluation of Teamwork (self and peer)
- Form 10.6, Evaluation of Project Management (self and teacher)
- Form 10.8, Perform Your Final Product and Evaluate Its Success (self)

- Form 12.1, Completed Integrated Project Checklist: Community Quilt
- Summary of audience evaluations

Teaching Required

- Oversee preparation of dedication celebration.
- Assist students with drafting brief descriptions that need to be inserted into form 10.10, Audience Evaluation of Project (description of project and assessment criteria).
- Arrange for refreshments.
- Have the event videotaped.
- Facilitate the student evaluation process after the dedication event. Students use the following evaluations to assess work:
  - Form 10.5, Evaluation of Teamwork (self and peer)
  - Form 10.6, Evaluation of Project Management (self)
  - Form 10.8, Perform Your Final Product and Evaluate Its Success (self)
- Summarize audience evaluations.
- Complete form 10.6, Evaluation of Project Management, for each student.

Materials Needed

- Form 10.5, Evaluation of Teamwork
- Form 10.6, Evaluation of Project Management

- Form 10.8, Perform Your Final Product and Evaluate Its Success
- Form 10.10, Audience Evaluation of Project
- Form 12.1, Integrated Project Checklist: Community Quilt
- Tape of performance, VCR, and TV
- One-page flyer or plain paper invitations

Suggested Time Frame

Six class periods (includes final preparations, performances, and post-performance evaluations).

Form 12.1　Student Worksheet—Integrated Project Checklist: Community Quilt (Grades 5 to 8)

Name _____ Class _____ Date _____

Instructions

Check off or have the teacher sign off on the following tasks as you complete them.

_____ 1. Inspiration activity

_____ 2. Dance designing activity

_____ 3. Research activity: selection of site

_____ 4. Research activity: development of questions

_____ 5. Research activity: documentation of interviewees and site

_____ 6. Conducting interviews

_____ 7. Major piece of work (quilt)

_____ 8. Major piece of work (dance)

_____ 9. Exhibition or culminating event

Form 12.1 Student Worksheet—Integrated Project Checklist: Community Quilt (Grades 5 to 8) from *Dance About Anything* by M. Sprague, H. Scheff, and S. McGreevy-Nichols, 2006, Champaign, IL: Human Kinetics.

Chapter 13

Prejudice and Human Rights: Anna and the King (Grades 9 to 12)

APPROPRIATE GRADE LEVEL

Grades 9 to 12.

CONTENT AREAS ADDRESSED

Dance, English language arts, applied learning, social studies.

FOCUSING OR GUIDING QUESTION

How can we create a dance production that clearly shows audiences how cultures and individuals can be made better by learning from other cultures and individuals?

PROJECT RATIONALE

When two cultures meet, a kind of mirror is held up to both cultures. Issues such as human rights and differences and similarities among people and their cultures are examined. People who meet when two cultures come together can change and grow. Our studies on Anna and the King point out the value of diversity.

MAJOR PIECE OF STUDENT WORK

Students create a dance production that illustrates the story Anna and the King and answers the focusing or guiding question.

EXHIBITION OR CULMINATING EVENT

Students participate in formal dance performances before audiences of elementary school students and the general public.

Student Work 1: Preproject Worksheets on Human Rights

Description of Student Work

Students develop an initial definition of the concept of human rights. The work includes reading different texts and completing worksheets.

Standards Met

- Social studies (human social systems and cultures)
- English language arts (writing, reading)

Student Instructions

1. Students write their first definition of human rights.
2. Students read various articles and texts on human rights and violations of human rights, complete **graphic organizers,** and share and discuss these texts.
3. Students write a second definition of the concept of human rights.

Rubric

- Above standard (+): Both definitions are complete and the second definition is more detailed and supported with examples taken from the readings. Each information area in the graphic organizer is completed for each reading.
- At standard (✓): Both definitions are complete and the second definition is more detailed. Each information area in the graphic organizer is completed for each reading.

Portfolio Evidence

- Preproject worksheet on human rights
- Graphic organizers for the information taken from the texts
- Form 13.1, Integrated Project Checklist: Anna and the King (shown at the end of the chapter and included on the CD-ROM)

Teaching Required

- Identify and gather appropriate articles and texts on human rights and violations of human rights.
- Create graphic organizers and worksheets for students to use as they gather information.
- Facilitate the reading activity and discussions.

Materials Needed

- Articles and texts on human rights and violations of human rights
- Graphic organizers and worksheets
- Form 13.1, Integrated Project Checklist: Anna and the King

Suggested Time Frame

One or two class periods.

Student Work 2: Inspiration Activity

Description of Student Work

 Students explore the Anna and the King Inspiration Activity (form 3.10). The work will include creating a movement phrase.

Standards Met

- Dance (critical and creative thinking, dance as communication)
- English language arts (reading)

Student Instructions

1. Students read and follow the instructions on form 3.10, Inspiration Activity Card: Anna and the King.
2. Students have their movement phrases videotaped.

Rubric

 Students create a movement phrase. No rubric is necessary. Inspiration Activity is checked off on form 13.1, Integrated Project Checklist: Anna and the King.

Portfolio Evidence

- Videotape of movement phrase
- Form 13.1, Integrated Project Checklist: Anna and the King

Teaching Required

- Facilitate Anna and the King Inspiration Activity (form 3.10).
- Videotape movement phrases.
- Using form 13.1, Integrated Project Checklist: Anna and the King, preview the entire integrated project with the students.

Materials Needed

- Form 3.3, How to Make Literal Movements Into Abstract Movements
- Form 3.10, Inspiration Activity Card: Anna and the King
- Form 13.1, Integrated Project Checklist: Anna and the King
- Video camera and blank tape; each activity would be recorded on one tape with all students. Individual student work is to be dubbed on their own video later.

Suggested Time Frame

One class period.

Student Work 3: Dance Designing Activity

Description of Student Work

Students create a dance that compares and contrasts two gestures, the Western handshake and the Siamese greeting shown in the films *Anna and the King* and *The King and I*. The dance should represent how two different cultures can interact in a friendly way.

Standards Met

- Dance (critical and creative thinking; choreographic structures, processes, and elements; dance as communication)
- Music (analysis of song structure)
- English language arts (analysis of media)
- Teamwork
- Social studies (cultural customs)

Student Instructions

1. Students participate in the Anna and the King Dance Designing Activity (form 6.10).
2. Students have both of their movement phrases of greeting gestures (Western and Siamese) videotaped. The videotape can be used to help the students decide on the best organization for the complete dance.
3. Students choose one of the suggestions for dance design to create the complete dance "Getting to Know You."

Rubric

Movement phrases (partner and group work) and the completed dance are videotaped.

- Above standard (+): Students have contributed 4 or more movement phrases to the dance. Students have designed transitions between sections of the dance.
- At standard (✓): Students have contributed 2 movement phrases (one based on the Western greeting and one based on the Siamese greeting) to the dance.

Portfolio Evidence

- Videotape of movement phrases (partner and group work) and the completed dance
- Form 13.1, Integrated Project Checklist: Anna and the King
- Videotape of the work

Teaching Required

- Model the choreographic (dance-making) process using the instructions in the dance designing activity.
- Facilitate the partner and group work and make dance suggestions based on form 3.3, How to Make Literal Movements Into Abstract Movements; form 4.1, Dance Ideas List; form 4.3, Choreographic Processes and Elements Resource Sheet; and form 4.4, Designing Movement Problems.
- Learn and teach the **hay** (grand right and left). (If you don't already know the hay, then a dance teacher or someone who knows how to square dance is a good resource for this information.) The hay is a group movement in which dancers weave in and out between each other. Equal numbers of dancers face one another and travel in opposite directions by passing one another's right shoulders (or hand clasps), then passing by the next person with their left shoulders (or hand clasps).
- Videotape the partner and group movement phrases and the complete dance.

Materials Needed

- Form 3.3, How to Make Literal Movements Into Abstract Movements
- Form 4.1, Dance Ideas List
- Form 4.3, Choreographic Processes and Elements Resource Sheet
- Form 4.4, Designing Movement Problems
- Form 6.10, Dance Designing Activity: Anna and the King
- Form 13.1, Integrated Project Checklist: Anna and the King
- Audio recording of "Getting to Know You" from the musical *The King and I*
- Parasols (Victorian and Asian)
- Video camera and blank tape
- Audio player

Suggested Time Frame

Four to six class periods.

Student Work 4: Research of Video Resources

Description of Student Work

Students complete graphic organizers based on viewing videos *Anna and the King, A&E Biography of Anna Leonowens* (Burns & Smith, 1998), and *The King and I.* The graphic organizers will be focused on identifying scenes that best portray issues of human rights and culture clash as well as character identification and development.

Standards Met

- English language arts (viewing, media)
- Social studies (human social structures, culture)
- Applied learning (gathering information for project)

Student Instructions

1. Students watch the videos and complete the graphic organizers to identify scenes that best portray issues of human rights and culture clash as well as character identification and development.
2. Students individually start to make decisions about which scenes should be included in the story line for the dance production.

Rubric

Students hand in graphic organizers. The completion of these graphic organizers or worksheets will be noted on form 13.1, Integrated Project Checklist: Anna and the King.

Portfolio Evidence

- Graphic organizers for research (viewing of videos)
- Form 13.1, Integrated Project Checklist: Anna and the King

Teaching Required

- Create graphic organizers to help students focus on and research identifying scenes that best portray issues of human rights and culture clash as well as character identification and development.
- Locate and show the videos *Anna and the King, A&E Biography of Anna Leonowens,* and *The King and I.*

- Instruct students on how to properly cite research sources. Refer to form 2.4, Bibliography Reference Sheet.

Materials Needed

- Graphic organizers
- Videos: *Anna and the King, A&E Biography of Anna Leonowens,* and *The King and I*
- VCR
- Form 2.4, Bibliography Reference Sheet
- Form 13.1, Integrated Project Checklist: Anna and the King

Suggested Time Frame

Six to eight class periods.

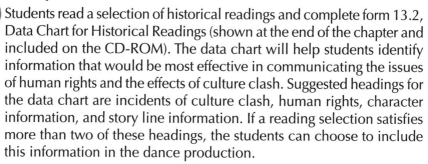

Student Work 5: Research of Historical Reading Selections

Description of Student Work

Students read a selection of historical readings and complete form 13.2, Data Chart for Historical Readings (shown at the end of the chapter and included on the CD-ROM). The data chart will help students identify information that would be most effective in communicating the issues of human rights and the effects of culture clash. Suggested headings for the data chart are incidents of culture clash, human rights, character information, and story line information. If a reading selection satisfies more than two of these headings, the students can choose to include this information in the dance production.

Standards Met

- English language arts (reading)
- Social studies (comparison of cultures)

Student Instructions

1. Students read a selection of historical readings.
2. For each reading, students mark the boxes under the headings that are addressed. (Note: There may be more than one box marked for each reading.)
3. Students identify the most important information in all of their readings and decide which readings would make the best dances for the production. (These decisions will be used in the next piece of student work.)

Rubric

Form 13.2, Data Chart for Historical Readings, will be completed and, after the next piece of work, will be filed as portfolio evidence. Completed data chart will be noted on form 13.1, Integrated Project Checklist: Anna and the King.

Portfolio Evidence

- Form 13.1, Integrated Project Checklist: Anna and the King
- Form 13.2, Data Chart for Historical Readings

Teaching Required

- Make available a wide selection of historical readings about Anna Leonowens' experiences in Siam that address culture clash, human rights, character information, and story line information.
- Create an instruction sheet or explain how to complete the assignment.
- Use reading strategies appropriate for the reading levels of students in the class.

Materials Needed

- A wide selection of historical readings about Anna Leonowens' experiences in Siam that address culture clash, human rights, character information, and story line information. The following are suggested resources:
  - Holland, C. (1999). *The story of Anna and the King.* New York: HarperCollins.
  - Landon, M. (2000). *Anna and the King of Siam.* New York: HarperPerennial.
  - Leonowens, A. (1999). *The English governess and the Siamese court.* New York: Tor.
- Form 13.1, Integrated Project Checklist: Anna and the King
- Form 13.2, Data Chart for Historical Readings

Suggested Time Frame

Three class periods.

Student Work 6: Persuasive Essay

Description of Student Work

Using the gathered information from the graphic organizers for the videos and form 13.2, Data Chart for Historical Readings, students write essays that describe important scenes or facts and persuade the reader that these scenes or facts should be included in the production.

Standards Met

- English language arts (persuasive writing, conventions, and grammar)
- Social studies (comparisons of cultures and traditions)
- Applied learning (gathering and analysis of information)

Student Instructions

1. Students review their research (graphic organizers and data chart) to identify scenes or facts that they want to include in the production.

2. Students write essays that describe important scenes or facts and persuade the reader that these scenes or facts should be included in the production. The essays should meet the particular English language arts expectations for the class or school. (The essays should be written as though the students were trying to convince producers to finance this production.)

Rubric

- Above standard (+): Choices of scenes or facts are explained with many supporting details. Writing effectively persuades the reader that the choices must be included in the production. There are ___ scenes or facts chosen and supported in the essay. (Teacher should fill in this number according to the amount of research resources used by the students.) Writing includes how and when the chosen scenes or facts will be used in the production.

- At standard (✓): Choices of scenes or facts are explained with details and a clear argument is made for inclusion in the production. There are ___ scenes or facts chosen and supported in the essay. (Teacher should fill in this number according to the amount of research resources used by the students.)

Portfolio Evidence

- Persuasive essay is included in the portfolio. (Graphic organizers and data chart should be filed in the portfolio at this time.)
- Form 13.1, Integrated Project Checklist: Anna and the King, is checked for the persuasive essay.

Teaching Required

- Either alone or with students, create a rubric for the persuasive essay for the selection of the scene or fact.
- Teach or review the components of an effective persuasive essay and the English language arts writing requirements. (If available, a sample of student writing will be helpful during this teaching or review.)

- Review proper citation of research sources. (Refer to form 2.4, Bibliography Reference Sheet.)
- Facilitate peer evaluations of the essays' rough drafts.

Materials Needed

- Students' completed graphic organizers for the videos and completed data charts (form 13.2) for the historical readings
- Persuasive writing sample and rubric
- Form 2.4, Bibliography Reference Sheet
- Form 13.1, Integrated Project Checklist: Anna and the King

Suggested Time Frame

One class period to teach and review and one week for students to complete final copy.

Student Work 7: Movement Problems

Description of Student Work

In small groups or individually, students write movement problems for movement phrases, dance sections, or complete dances. This is to be done for each of the scenes chosen from the persuasive essays, unless the teacher or a guest artist is choreographing some of the dances or scenes.

Standards Met

- Dance (critical and creative thinking; choreographic structures, processes, and elements; world dance forms; movement skills)
- Social studies (culture and traditions)
- Applied learning (teamwork)

Student Instructions

The following instructions apply to each dance and movement problem:

1. Students complete any worksheets given to them. These worksheets will help them devise their movement problems.
2. From the research, students choose the main idea of the dance and smaller ideas to be included.

3. Students choose from form 4.1, Dance Ideas List, appropriate movement and dance ideas and choreographic structures, processes, and elements.
4. Students choose the procedure (what should be done and in what order) to be used by the dancers who will be solving the movement problem.
5. Students write a final copy of the movement problem.

Rubric

Teacher fills in the number of movement problems each student should write based on the size of the production.

- Above standard (+): Student has contributed at least __ movement problems for the creation of movement phrases or dance sections. Student has written movement problem(s) for complete dance(s) for the production.
- At standard (✓): Student has contributed at least __ movement problems for the creation of movement phrases or dance sections for the dances in the production.

Portfolio Evidence

- Worksheets
- Written movement problems

- Form 13.1, Integrated Project Checklist: Anna and the King

Teaching Required

- Teach or review the dance and choreographic concepts needed in order to complete a movement problem.
- Choose the appropriate student worksheet(s) to help students devise their movement problems (see the forms listed below in Materials Needed).
- Facilitate the writing of the movement problems.

Materials Needed

- Form 3.3, How to Make Literal Movements Into Abstract Movements
- Form 4.1, Dance Ideas List
- Form 4.2, Choreographic Structures Resource Sheet
- Form 4.3, Choreographic Processes and Elements Resource Sheet
- Form 4.4, Designing Movement Problems
- Form 13.1, Integrated Project Checklist: Anna and the King

Suggested Time Frame

At least one class period per dance.

Student Work 8: Movement Solutions

Description of Student Work

For each dance, students solve the movement problems, thereby constructing dance sections or complete dances. Students then evaluate and revise the dances as necessary.

Standards Met

- Dance (critical and creative thinking; choreographic structures, processes, and elements; world dance forms; movement skills)
- Social studies (culture and traditions)
- Applied learning (teamwork)

Student Instructions

The following instructions apply for each dance:

1. In small groups, or as dictated by the instructions in the movement problems, students solve the movement problems, thereby constructing dance sections or complete dances.

2. Students reflect on solving the movement problems (using form 5.3, Reflection on Solving the Movement Problem).

3. If students have made dance sections, they will organize them into complete dances. Students can use form 5.4, Playing With Your Movement Phrase or Dance Section, and form 5.5, Putting It All Together, to help them construct complete dances.

4. Students' dances are videotaped.

5. Using form 5.1, Evaluating What Works and What Does Not Work, and form 5.2, Self-Evaluation of Work, students evaluate their dances and make any needed revisions.

Rubric

Teacher fills in the number of movement solutions each student should solve based on the size of the production.

- Above standard (+): All of the criteria for at-standard work, plus student has individually organized (crafted) dance sections from movement solutions to make ___ complete dance(s).

- At standard (✓): Student has solved at least ___ movement problems and has constructed dance section(s) for at least ___ dances in the production.

Portfolio Evidence

- Form 5.1, Evaluating What Works and What Does Not Work
- Form 5.2, Self-Evaluation of Work
- Form 5.3, Reflection on Solving the Movement Problem
- Form 5.4, Playing With Your Movement Phrase or Dance Section

- Form 5.5, Putting It All Together
- Form 13.1, Integrated Project Checklist: Anna and the King
- Videotapes of dance sections and dances

Teaching Required

- Facilitate the solving of the movement problems, designing of the dances, and evaluating and revision process.
- Teach or review needed concepts and skills for the choreographic process.
- Videotape the dances.

Materials Needed

- Form 5.1, Evaluating What Works and What Does Not Work
- Form 5.2, Self-Evaluation of Work

- Form 5.3, Reflection on Solving the Movement Problem
- Form 5.4, Playing With Your Movement Phrase or Dance Section
- Form 5.5, Putting It All Together
- Form 13.1, Integrated Project Checklist: Anna and the King
- Music scores from films and musicals of *Anna and the King* and music from Thailand
- Video camera and blank tape; each activity would be recorded on one tape with all students. Individual student work is to be dubbed on their own video later.

Suggested Time Frame

About four class periods per dance.

Student Work 9: Major Piece of Work

Description of Student Work

Students place the dances in the order of the story line, practice, evaluate the entire production, and revise any part of the production as needed.

Standards Met

- Dance (critical and creative thinking; choreographic structures, processes, and elements; world dance forms; performance of movement skills)
- Social studies (culture and traditions)
- Applied learning (teamwork)

Student Instructions

1. Students memorize and practice dances.
2. Students organize the dances in an order that makes sense with the story line.
3. Students have a run-through (rehearsal) videotaped.
4. Students create the description of project and criteria for assessment for form 10.10, Audience Evaluation of Project.
5. Students refine their personal performance and the production based on self-evaluation, peer evaluation, teacher evaluation, and perhaps a critique from a small invited audience.

Rubric

- Above standard (+): All of the at-standard criteria, plus student takes on the role of dance captain (person in charge of maintaining the quality of performance of a dance) for one or more dances.
- At standard (✓): Student completes the following: a personal practice log (list of dates and amount of time documenting practice sessions); written suggestions for improvements in the performance of individual dances and the whole production (for self and the whole cast); and evaluation of the production using form 10.8, Perform Your Final Product and Evaluate Its Success, and form 10.10, Audience Evaluation of Project.

Portfolio Evidence

- Video of the rehearsals of the production
- Personal practice log
- Written suggestions for improvements in the performance of individual dances and the whole production (for self and the whole cast)

- Form 10.8, Perform Your Final Product and Evaluate Its Success
- Form 10.10, Audience Evaluation of Project
- Form 13.1, Integrated Project Checklist: Anna and the King

Teaching Required

- Create a personal practice log. (A calendar page works well. Require the signature of a parent or guardian on the document to verify that the student practiced at home.)
- Facilitate discussion of order of dances for the story line.
- Coach rehearsals.
- Facilitate critiques.
- Videotape the rehearsals.

Materials Needed

- Personal practice log
- Form 10.8, Perform Your Final Product and Evaluate Its Success
- Form 10.10, Audience Evaluation of Project
- Form 13.1, Integrated Project Checklist: Anna and the King
- Video camera and blank tapes

Suggested Time Frame

Two to three weeks (maybe more), depending on the size of the production.

Student Work 10: Exhibition or Culminating Event

Description of Student Work
Students participate in formal dance performances before audiences of elementary school students and the general public.

Standards Met
- Dance (critical and creative thinking; choreographic structures, processes, and elements; world dance forms; performance of movement skills)
- Social studies (culture and traditions)
- Applied learning (teamwork)

Student Instructions
1. Students perform the production for students and the general public.

2. After the event, students watch the videotape and complete final evaluations and reflections. To do this work, use the following worksheets: form 10.5, Evaluation of Teamwork (self and a peer); form 10.6, Evaluation of Project Management (self); form 10.8, Perform Your Final Product and Evaluate Its Success (self).

Rubric
Evaluating the whole project

Above Standard (+)
- Student completes all tasks of the project.
- Portfolio evidence, including self-evaluations, peer evaluations, and teacher evaluations, is completed with at least 75% of the work rated at above standard.
- Student takes part in the final performance.
- Student demonstrates a high quality of reflection in the final evaluation process by submitting a reflective essay that includes the following content:
  1. a discussion of research activities and assignments;
  2. a discussion of student choreography assignments (inspiration activities, dance designing activities, writing and solving movement problems, and organizing complete dances);

3. a discussion about learning and performing dances choreographed by teachers or guest artists; and

4. personal observations about the performances and the success of the final production, including suggestions for possible improvements.

- Student volunteers to take on responsibilities above and beyond what is required.

At Standard (✓)

- All tasks of the project are completed.
- Portfolio evidence, including self-evaluations, peer evaluations, and teacher evaluations, is graded at standard.
- Student takes part in final performance.

Portfolio Evidence

- Video of the performance
- Form 10.5, Evaluation of Teamwork (self and peer)
- Form 10.6, Evaluation of Project Management
- Form 10.8, Perform Your Final Product and Evaluate Its Success (self)
- Form 10.10, Audience Evaluation of Project
- Form 13.1, Integrated Project Checklist: Anna and the King

Teaching Required

- Coach students during the performance of the production
- Oversee the entire exhibition or event
- Videotape the performance.

Materials Needed

- Form 10.5, Evaluation of Teamwork (self and peer)
- Form 10.6, Evaluation of Project Management
- Form 10.8, Perform Your Final Product and Evaluate Its Success (self)
- Form 10.10, Audience Evaluation of Project
- Form 13.1, Integrated Project Checklist: Anna and the King
- Video camera and blank tapes

Suggested Time Frame

One or more performances and two or three class periods for final evaluation.

Form 13.1 Student Worksheet—Integrated Project Checklist: Anna and the King (Grades 9 to12)

Name _____ Class _____ Date _____

Instructions

Check off or have the teacher sign off on the following tasks as you complete them.

_____ 1. Preproject worksheets on human rights

_____ 2. Inspiration activity

_____ 3. Dance designing activity

_____ 4. Research of video resources

_____ 5. Research of historical reading selections

_____ 6. Persuasive essay

_____ 7. Movement problems

_____ 8. Movement solutions

_____ 9. Major piece of work

_____ 10. Exhibition or culminating event

Form 13.1 Student Worksheet—Integrated Project Checklist: Anna and the King (Grades 9 to 12) from *Dance About Anything* by M. Sprague, H. Scheff, and S. McGreevy-Nichols, 2006, Champaign, IL: Human Kinetics.

Form 13.2 Student Worksheet—Data Chart for Historical Readings

Name _____ Class _____ Date _____

Instructions

For each reading, check the appropriate box for the issues and aspects that are addressed.

Reading number	Culture clash	Human rights	Character information	Story line information
1				
2				
3				
4				
5				
6				
7				
8				
9				
10				
11				
12				
13				
14				
15				
16				
17				
18				
19				
20				
21				
22				
23				

Form 13.2 Student Worksheet—Data Chart for Historical Readings from *Dance About Anything* by M. Sprague, H. Scheff, and S. McGreevy-Nichols, 2006, Champaign, IL: Human Kinetics.

Glossary

AB—Can be described as A (a dance phrase) and B (a new dance phrase).

ABA—Can be described as A (a dance phrase), B (a new dance phrase), and a return to A (the first dance phrase).

abstract movement—Movement that differs from but is still loosely based on the literal movement.

accumulation—A choreographic form that can be described by the following model: (1), (1, 2), (1, 2, 3), (1, 2, 3, 4), (1, 2, 3, 4, 5). If each number represents a distinct movement or dance phrase, then it is clear that this structure is constructed by adding on different movement or dance phrases.

air patterns—Dancers' pathways in the air as they move through space.

asymmetrical shapes and formations—Shapes and formations that are different on both sides of a centerline. For example, in an asymmetrical formation there would be an unequal number of dancers on each side of the centerline of the stage. There could be one dancer on one side and four on the other side.

beginning, middle, and end—A structure basic to all the choreographic structures. A dance should have a beginning shape or pose or entrance, a middle consisting of development or exploration of the main idea, and a clear end consisting of a shape or pose or exit.

block booking—When several schools within a district come to the show, or several classes within a school come to the same performance.

call and response—A choreographic form that can be described as conversational: One person moves and the other person's movement responds to (answers) the movement of the initial mover, just as in a tap challenge.

canon—Also known as a round. Two or more movement parts are involved in a composition in which the main movement is imitated exactly and completely by the successive movements.

chance dance—A choreographic form that can be described as a series of dance phrases performed in a random order. Each time the dance is done, it is in a different order and therefore has a different appearance.

choreographic elements—Elements that organize the dancer in the dance, manipulate the movement, and guide the audience's attention.

choreographic processes—Methods used to enhance and carry the dance forward.

choreographic structures—Forms that organize movement in a dance.

coaching—A teaching style in which the teacher only observes, encourages, and provides suggestions to improve student performance.

cognitive processes—Thinking processes.

collage—A choreographic form that consists of a series of movement phrases that are often unrelated but have been brought together to create a single dance with a beginning, a middle, and an end.

complementary—A choreographic process that involves developing different but related shapes, movements, or movement phrases. For example, make a shape out of curves. Then make a different shape, but still use curves. It is as though the complementary shapes, movements, or movement phrases were "cousins" to the original shapes, movements, or movement phrases. They are similar, but not precisely the same.

contrast—A choreographic process that adds interest through developing opposite shapes, movements, or movement phrases. For example, if you have a shape made of angles, you would then make a shape using curves for contrast.

copying—A choreographic process in which the choreographer repeats an already-existing shape, movement, or movement phrase at a later time in the dance or in a different space on the stage.

critique—Observations, corrections, and comments.

cue-to-cue rehearsal—A rehearsal that involves running the music, sound, curtain, and light cues from the beginning of the show to the final curtain, usually without the dancers.

direct teaching—Teacher instructs, the student learns, and then students' learning is tested.

duet—Two persons dancing at one time.

effort actions (Laban)—Combinations of three effort elements:

- dab—Uses light weight, sudden time, and direct space.
- flick—Uses light weight, sudden time, and indirect space.
- float—Uses light weight, sustained time, and indirect space.
- glide—Uses light weight, sustained time, and direct space.
- press—Uses strong weight, sustained time, and direct space.
- punch—Uses strong weight, sudden time, and direct space.
- slash—Uses strong weight, sudden time, and indirect space.
- wring—Uses strong weight, sustained time, and indirect space.

effort elements (Laban)—The attitudes toward the energy that is exerted when doing a movement:

- flow—Attitude toward flow is bound (controlled) or free (uncontrolled).
- space—Attitude toward space is direct (the movement has a single focus) or indirect (the movement has many foci).
- time—Attitude toward time is sudden (showing urgency or anxiety) or sustained (showing a relaxed, easygoing feeling).
- weight—Attitude toward weight is strong (expending much energy) or light (using a fine or delicate touch).

ensemble—A group of people dancing at one time.

facilitating—A teaching style in which the teacher steps back from the lead in the teaching and learning process. Guiding, prompting, and encouraging are the main instructional activities.

facings—The stage directions to which dancers perform their movements.

floor patterns—Dancers' pathways on the floor as they move through space.

focal point—When the choreographer designs the movement and spacing in such a way that the choreography dictates where the audience will look.

graphic organizers—Worksheets that visually organize information.

ground bass—Choreographic structure like the backup singers in a singing group. A group of dancers repeats a series of simple movements while, in front, fewer dancers (or a soloist) perform a contrasting, often more complex, dance phrase.

groupings and formations—Where dancers stand in relation to other dancers.

hay (grand right and left)—Group movement in which dancers weave in and out between each other. Equal numbers of dancers face each other and travel in opposite directions by passing by each others' right shoulders (or hand clasps) then passing by the next person with their left shoulders (or hand clasps). The hay is usually done in a circle formation, but it can also be performed in a line.

improvisation—Movement done without planning.

integrate—To bring together or incorporate (parts) into a whole.

integrated project—Units in which various subject areas are brought together and the learning is approached as a whole.

level—Where the body is in space; can be described as high, middle, and low.

literal movement—The exact, real-life movement. For example, a handshake is a literal movement.

locomotor movement—Traveling movement.

motif and development—A choreographic form that can be described as a brief movement phrase that is danced and then developed into a full-blown dance or section of a dance.

movement phrases—"Sentences" composed of movement.

movement prompt—A prompt that encourages students to explore an idea through improvised movement; similar to a writing prompt.

movement qualities—Can be both performed and perceived as smooth, swing, percussive, collapse, or vibratory.

movement signature—An identifying movement or short series of movements.

movement skills—Made up of locomotor and nonlocomotor movements.

movement solution—Movement phrase or answer to the movement problem.

moving definition—Movement that expresses the meaning of a word.

moving image—An idea, topic, concept, emotion, or story line communicated through movement.

narrative—A choreographic form that tells a story or conveys an idea. The sequence of the story determines the structure of the dance.

nonlocomotor movement—Movement that stays in place. Also called *axial movement.*

partnering and weight sharing—Guiding, giving, and taking weight from another dancer.

prior knowledge—Skills and knowledge that a person already has.

process portfolio—A portfolio that provides documentation of the evidence of student thinking, reflection, and learning throughout the various steps of the project.

repetition—A movement or movement pattern that is repeated.

rondo—Can be described as ABACADA. The choreographic pattern begins with a main theme (A) followed by another theme or movement material, and the A theme returns after each new movement phrase.

silence—In dance, the absence of movement. To illustrate, a dancer holding a shape is demonstrating silence.

size of movement—Large or small movement.

solo—One person dancing.

strike—To break down or take apart the scenery, props, and costumes after a show.

suite—A choreographic form that uses different tempos and qualities in each of its three or more sections. Usually the first section is a moderate tempo, the second is an adagio (slow tempo), and the last section is an allegro (fast tempo).

symmetrical shapes and formations—Shapes and formations that are the same on both sides of a centerline. For example, in a symmetrical formation there would be an equal number of dancers on each side of the centerline of the stage. Both sides of the stage would look the same.

tempo—Speed of the movements.

theme and variation—Can be described as a dance phrase or section of a dance with subsequent dance phrases or sections being variations of the original. This would be A, A1, A2, A3.

transition—Movement that connects one movement or movement phrase to the next movement or movement phrase. For example, if a movement at a low level is followed by a movement at a high level, you can insert a transitional movement at the middle level.

trio—Three people dancing at one time.

unison—When the dancers are all moving at the same time and doing the same movement in the same way.

variety—Within the dance, different movements and patterns are used.

Venn diagram—A graphic organizer in which two circles intersect; usually used to make comparisons between concepts with the center section used to place aspects that both concepts share.

visualization reading strategy—Seeing images in your mind as you read words and sentences.

References

American Psychological Association. (2001). *Publication manual of the American Psychological Association* (5th ed.). Washington, DC: American Psychological Association.

Arnheim, R. (1983). Perceiving, thinking, forming. *Art Education, 36*(2), 9-11.

Brackett, C. (Producer), & Lang, W. (Director). (1956). *The King and I.* [Motion picture]. Los Angeles: 20th Century Fox.

Breeden, S. (1988, February). The first Australians. *National Geographic, 173*(2), 276-279.

Burns, K. (Producer), & Smith, S. (Director). (1998). *A&E Biography of Anna Leonowens.* [Motion Picture]. United States: Arts and Entertainment.

Dewey, J. (1934). *Art as experience.* New York: Putnam.

Dynamic Flight, Inc. (1999-2004). Basic aerodynamics. Available: www.dynamicflight.com/aerodynamics/basics. Accessed September 5, 2005.

Eisner, E. (1982). *On cognition and curriculum: A basis for deciding what to teach.* New York: Longman.

Gardner, H. (1999). *Intelligence reframed: Multiple intelligences for the 21st century.* New York: Basic Books.

Hannaford, C. (1995). *Smart moves: Why learning is not all in your head.* Arlington, VA: Great Ocean.

Holland, C. (1999). *The story of Anna and the king.* New York: HarperCollins.

Jashni, J., McCormick, K. (Producers), & Tennant, A. (Director). (1999). *Anna and the king.* [Motion Picture]. Los Angeles: 20th Century Fox.

Jensen, E. (1998). *Teaching with the brain in mind.* Alexandria, VA: Association for Supervision and Curriculum Development.

Landon, M. (2000). *Anna and the king of Siam.* New York: HarperPerennial.

Ledoux, J. (1996). *The emotional brain: The mysterious underpinnings of emotional life.* New York: Simon & Schuster.

Leonowens, A. (1999). *The English governess and the Siamese court.* New York: Tor.

Lyons, W. (1997). *The handy weather answer book.* Canton, MI: Visible Ink Press.

McGreevy-Nichols, S., Scheff, H., & Sprague, M. (2001). *Building more dances.* Champaign, IL: Human Kinetics.

McGreevy-Nichols, S., Scheff, H., & Sprague, M. (2005). *Building dances (2nd ed.).* Champaign, IL: Human Kinetics.

Perkins, D.N. (1989). Selecting fertile themes for integrated learning. In Jacobs, H.H. (Ed.), *Interdisciplinary curriculum: Design and implementation.* Alexandria, VA: Association for Supervision and Curriculum Development.

Ringgold, F., Freeman, L., & Roucher, N. (1996). *Talking to Faith Ringgold.* New York: Crown Books.

Rogers, R., & Hammerstein, O. (1987). The king and I. [CD]. USA: Capitol Records.

Scheff, H., Sprague, M., & McGreevy-Nichols, S. (2005). *Experiencing dance: From student to dance artist.* Champaign, IL: Human Kinetics.

Scheff, H., Sprague, M., & McGreevy-Nichols, S. (2005). *Experiencing dance: From student to dance artist instructor guide.* Champaign, IL: Human Kinetics.

Secretary's Commission on Achieving Necessary Skills. (1991). *What work requires of schools.* Washington, DC: U.S. Department of Labor.

Sherman, R.M., & Sherman, R.B. (1995). *Take my hand: Songs from the 100 acre wood.* [CD]. Burbank, CA: Walt Disney Records.

Sylwester, R. (2000). *A biological brain in a cultural classroom: Applying biological research to classroom management.* Thousand Oaks, CA: Corwin Press.

Wolfe, P. (2001). *Brain matters: Translating research into classroom practice.* Alexandria, VA: Association for Supervision and Curriculum Development.

About the Authors

Marty Sprague, MA, is a professional choreographer and performer with more than 29 years of experience in public dance education. She is the dance teacher at the Providence Academy of International Studies and artistic director of Chance to Dance.

Marty holds a master's degree in dance education from Teachers College at Columbia University and a BFA in dance from Boston Conservatory. She has been a licensed trainer for the National Center for Education and the Economy's Course I, Standards-Based Curriculum (a professional development course for standards-based teaching and learning). She served on the Rhode Island Governor's Task Force for Literacy in the Arts. Marty is a member of the Arabella Project, a dance group exploring the realms of the older dancer.

Marty is coauthor of *Building Dances: A Guide to Putting Movements Together, Second Edition* (2005); *Building More Dances: Blueprints for Putting Movements Together* (2001); and *Experiencing Dance: From Student to Dance Artist* (2005). She also served as a consultant to the authors for the first edition of *Building Dances: A Guide to Putting Movements Together* (1995).

In 1992 and 2005 Marty was named the Rhode Island Dance Educator of the Year and in 1998 earned an Outstanding Professional Award from EDA (Eastern District Association). In 2004, Marty was honored with *Dance Teacher* Magazine's Dance Teacher of the Year Award for K-12. National Dance Education Organization honored her as the Outstanding Dance Educator K-12 in October 2005. She is a member of the National Dance Association (NDA) and the Association for Supervision and Curriculum Development, and she is a charter member of National Dance Education Organization (NDEO).

Helene Scheff, RDE, has been a dance educator and administrator for 45 years in both the public and private sectors. She is coauthor of the first and second editions of *Building Dances: A Guide to Putting Movements Together* (1995 and 2005), *Building More Dances: Blueprints for Putting Movements Together* (2001), and *Experiencing Dance: From Student to Dance Artist* (2005).

A registered dance educator, Helene is the founder and executive director of Chance to Dance, an in-school dance program started in 1985 that brings quality dance education to children in grades 4 through 8.

A graduate of the famed NYC High School of Performing Arts, Helene is a former dancer with the Joffrey Ballet. She is a founding member and former president of the Dance Alliance of Rhode Island and has served as vice president of dance for the Eastern District Association (EDA) of the American Alliance for Health, Physical Education, Recreation and Dance. She is a board member of the Rhode Island Alliance for Arts Education and the Committee Liaison for UNITY. Helene is a member of the National Dance Association (NDA) and dance and the Child international (daCi), and she is a charter member of the National Dance Education Organization (NDEO).

Helene was named the Rhode Island Association for Health, Physical Education, Recreation and Dance's (RIAHPERD) Dance Teacher of the Year in 1996 and was honored as an EDA Outstanding Professional in 1996. She received the RIAHPERD President's Honor Award in 1997 and an NDA Presidential Citation in 1998. She was awarded the Dance Alliance of Rhode Island Dance Legacy Award in 2002. Most recently she was given the Meritorious Service Award by RIAHPERD in 2005.

Susan McGreevy-Nichols is a national arts education consultant. She teaches part-time at California State University at Dominguez Hills. She taught at Roger Williams Middle School in Providence, Rhode Island, from 1974 to 2002. She was the founder and director of the inner-city school's nationally recognized dance program in which more than 300 of the school's 900 students elected to participate.

Susan is coauthor of the first and second editions of *Building Dances: A Guide to Putting Movements Together* (1995 and 2005), *Building More Dances: Blueprints for Putting Movements Together* (2001), and *Experiencing Dance: From Student to Dance Artist* (2005). She is a charter member and presenter of the National Dance Education Organization (NDEO) and a former treasurer and board member. She also has served as the president of the National Dance Association (NDA) and the nominating chair and Rhode Island state leader for the Kennedy Center Alliance for Arts Education. She is currently the co-president of the California Dance Education Association.

Susan has received numerous NDA presidential citations and an Eastern District Association (EDA) of the American Alliance of Health, Physical Education, Recreation and Dance (AAHPERD) Merit Award in Dance. In 1994 she was named Rhode Island's Dance Teacher of the Year, and in 1995 she was honored both as the NDA National Dance Teacher of the Year and as an EDA Outstanding Professional. She received AAHPERD's Honor Award in 2000. Susan resides in Santa Monica, California.

CD-ROM Quick-Start Instructions

Minimum System Requirements

The *Dance About Anything CD-ROM* can be used on either a Windows®-based PC or a Macintosh computer.

Windows

- IBM PC compatible with Pentium® processor
- Windows® 98/NT 4.0/2000/ME/XP
- Adobe Acrobat Reader®
- At least 16 MB RAM with 32 MB recommended
- 4x CD-ROM drive
- Inkjet or laser printer (optional)
- 256 colors
- Mouse

Macintosh

- Power Mac® recommended
- System 9.x or higher
- Adobe Acrobat Reader®
- At least 16 MB RAM with 32 MB recommended
- 4x CD-ROM drive
- Inkjet or laser printer (optional)
- 256 colors
- Mouse

User Instructions

Windows

1. Insert the *Dance About Anything CD-ROM*. (*Note:* The CD-ROM must be present in the drive at all times.) The CD-ROM should launch automatically. If not, proceed to step 2.
2. Select the "My Computer" icon from the desktop.
3. Select the CD-ROM drive.
4. Open the "Start.htm" file.
5. Follow the instructions on screen.

Macintosh

1. Insert the *Dance About Anything CD-ROM*. (*Note:* The CD-ROM must be present in the drive at all times.)
2. Double-click the CD icon located on the desktop.
3. Open the "Start" file.
4. Follow the instructions on screen.

Note: OSX users, you must first open Acrobat Reader®, then select the file you wish to view from your CD-ROM drive and open the file from within Acrobat Reader®. For MacOS 10.1 and 10.2, you may need to be in Classic mode for the links on the table of contents to work correctly.

For product information or customer support:
E-mail: support@hkusa.com
Phone: 217-351-5076 (ext. 2970)
Fax: 217-351-2674

Web site: **www.HumanKinetics.com**